MAX FACTOR'S HOLLYWOOD
GLAMOUR · MOVIES · MAKE-UP

BY FRED E. BASTEN

WITH ROBERT SALVATORE & PAUL A. KAUFMAN

Publisher: W. Quay Hays
Editor: Peter Hoffman
Art Director: Susan Anson
Assistant Art Director: Maritta Tapanainen
Production Director: Nadeen Torio
Color and Prepress Director: Gaston Moraga
Production Assistants: Michael Lira, Tom Archibeque, Alan Peak, Brad Slepack

The authors wish to thank Procter & Gamble Company for providing access to
the Max Factor Museum Archives. We are also deeply indebted to the Max Factor
Family Foundation.

"Academy Award(s)®" and "Oscar®" are registered trademarks and service marks
of the Academy of Motion Picture Arts and Sciences (A.M.P.A.S.).

"Hooray for Hollywood" by Richard A. Whiting and Johnny Mercer, © 1937, 1938
(renewed) Warner Bros. Inc. All rights reserved. Used by permission. Warner Bros.
Publications, Inc., Miami, FL 33014.

Library of Congress Catalog Card Number: 95-080699
ISBN: 1-881649-06-7

Printed in the USA
10 9 8 7 6 5 4 3 2 1

General Publishing Group
Los Angeles

Table of Contents

Acknowledgments

The authors wish to thank the following individuals and organizations for their invaluable contributions to this book:

Joe Alba	Missouri Historical Society
Shari Belafonte	Jay Morganstern
Barbara Factor Bentley	Dave Olsen
Joseph Bentley	Procter & Gamble Co.
Boyle Heights Chamber of Commerce	Keith W. Raistrick
Deborah Brown	Ed Rider
Joe Buissink	Josephine Salvatore
Ralph Carmona	Leo Salvatore
Amy Fischer	Jane Seymour
Noreen Hinds	Josephine Turner
Huell Howser	Fran Tygell
Betty Jennings	Neil Van Scoten
Shari L. Kaufman	Jeanne Veloz
Randy Koss	Barbara Whiting
Rhonda Fleming Mann	Margaret Whiting
Max Factor Family Foundation	Sophia Xixis

Introduction

Late one night, my wife, Shari, and I were watching television, channel surfing, and we came across a show about The Max Factor Museum on PBS. We love Hollywood history and were instantly hooked. Growing up in Los Angeles in the 1970s, I knew the name "Max Factor." It was the make-up of the time, as well as the make-up my mother and sister used. What I didn't know, and soon learned, was that Max Factor was much more than just a product. Max Factor was the force behind what we know today as "glamour" and "beauty."

Max Factor literally changed the look of women around the world by creating glamorous looks and theatrical make-up for the stars during Hollywood's Golden Era, including Marlene Dietrich, Judy Garland, Jean Harlow, Lucille Ball and Greta Garbo to name a few. Once the public saw the actresses looking so glamorous and beautiful on screen, they wanted to look just like them.

The more I discovered about the genius of Max Factor and his dynasty, the more I became enchanted with his story. I wanted to share my newfound knowledge, which led to my directing a short documentary about him. This in turn brought Robert Salvatore, Fred Basten and me together to produce this wonderful book. In the following chapters, you will discover Max Factor's fascinating world of make-up for the movies, and the glamorous women of Hollywood—and the world.

—*Paul A. Kaufman*

Hooray for Hollywood.
You may be homely in your neighborhood,
But if you think that you can be an actor,
See Mr. Factor.
He'd make a monkey look good.
Within a half an hour
You'll look like Tyrone Power.
Hooray for Hollywood.

...from Hollywood Hotel, 1937
words by Johnny Mercer
music by Richard A. Whiting

Max Factor in uniform during his four-year service in the Russian Army, starting in 1890.

Chapter 1

The Journey

Even as a youngster Max displayed extraordinary ability. By his eighth birthday, he was serving as apprentice to a doctor's assistant. Within the next few years he was learning the art of constructing hairpieces from a wigmaker in his hometown. It was his flair for creating beauty that attracted attention and, before long, he was in the service of royalty.

M ax Faktor, the future Max Factor, was born in Lodz, Poland, to Abraham and Cecilia Tandowsky Faktor. The exact year of his birth was never verified. Even Max, in his later years, was not certain, although 1872, 1874 and 1877 were the dates most reported. Given the events that crowded his young life, 1872 appears to be the most accurate.

The Faktors were a humble Jewish family. In addition to Max, there were nine other children in the household. Hard times outnumbered the good, which made it difficult for them to afford a formal education for any of their children. And, like many other struggling families, the youngsters began to serve apprenticeships with local merchants. For Max, it was acting as an assistant, or "felcher," to a dentist-apothecary, a man who not only provided dental care but supplied remedies, potions and pills to the sick and ailing. No ordinary eight year old would last long in such an atmosphere. But it was during this apprenticeship that Max's young eyes were first introduced to the wonders—and beauty—of the human body.

It was several years later that Max became an apprentice to a wigmaker in Lodz. Here he would learn to tie and weave human hair onto silken foundations. While most other little boys were playing jackstraws and skating, Max was learning a trade he would follow the rest of his life.

When he was 14 he got his first paying job. The Imperial Russian Grand Opera hired him as a wigmaker, make-up artist and costumer, but he was also prop boy, errand man, hairdresser, valet and all-around whipping post. If the evening's performance did not go well, the tenor blamed Max's make-up. If the basso misplaced his score, it was because Max had kept him waiting. As for the diva, perhaps Max hadn't arched her eyebrows to her liking on the night when the Czar was in the audience.

Max took all the blame and kept on learning, at least until his 18th birthday, when he joined the Russian Army for four years, as was required by law. He had hoped to become involved with military dramatics, but that wasn't to be. "The first day they picked me for the Hospital Corps," he later

Earliest known photo of Max Factor (then Faktor), shown here at age 16 in 1888. The teenager was then working as a wigmaker and cosmetician for the Imperial Russian Grand Opera Company.

Formally dressed audiences attending performances at the Art Theater of Moscow were among the first to see Max Factor's mastery of make-up.

In 1894, after serving four years in the military, Max Factor (right, at doorway) returned to Russia where he opened his first hairgoods/cosmetics shop in the town of R'azan.

recalled, "the doctor prescribed and I did the work. I did not like it, but I absorbed much." What he absorbed was how to bleed patients with cups and leeches, and all he wanted to know about was phrenology and skin disorders.

Upon his release from the Army in 1894, Max opened a small shop off the town square in R'azan, a suburb of Moscow. There he made and sold his own creams, rouges, fragrances and wigs. According to one story, a traveling theatrical troupe had stopped at Max's shop while passing through R'azan. Members of the company had purchased Max's make-up, which they wore while entertaining the Imperial family. It wasn't easy to impress royalty, but soon after Max counted among his clientele the summer court of Russian nobility.

Whether the theatrical troupe had a hand in Max's sudden good fortune is impossible to know, but his business suddenly took a royal upswing. From then on, his young life was never the same.

Max's services were more than simply engaged by the Russian nobility, they were commanded. He was given the title of cosmetic expert not only to Alexander Nicolaivich Romanoff, uncle to Czar Nicholas II, but also to the Czar's personal physician and the Imperial Russian Grand Opera.

Depiction showing the crowning of Nicholas II in the Kremlin's Ouspensky Cathedral. The gilded splendor of such surroundings, and life within the royal court, were early influences on Max Factor's lifelong infatuation with beauty.

Visits to the summer palace and its elegant gardens were part of Max Factor's itinerary as cosmetician to the Imperial family.

Czar Nicholas II and the Imperial family. (The missing daughter of Czar Nicholas II of Russia, who had supposedly escaped death in the 1918 assassination of the Royal Family, was the basis of the hit Broadway play and subsequent motion picture, *Anastasia*, which won a best actress award for Ingrid Bergman in 1956.)

Life should have been wonderful for Max, but it wasn't. He had security, recognition, money, everything that seemed important. He didn't mind kowtowing to the often demanding aristocracy of the court or creating a new style of hair for the Grand Duchess. He didn't mind bowing to the divas of the opera. What bothered him was his lack of freedom. "I was like a slave," he said, years later. "I had no life. A dozen people were always watching me, following me. I could see no one on my own. I was allowed only to make the court handsome. I had nothing for myself."

Actually, Max did have something secret in his life—only he couldn't talk about it because he was forbidden to court a woman, to love or to marry. Her name was Esther Rosa, but Max called her Lizzie. The slight, dark-haired young girl had first wandered into Max's shop in R'azan to select perfume shortly after his release from the Army. Her visits were limited only to once a week, but she returned again and again. According to the strict ruling of the Czar's uncle, Max was allowed to leave the palace every seventh day, always with a guard. And so the young lady from Moscow would slip into the back door of a friend's house on the given day. Max would enter the front door with his make-up kit, supposedly on business, while the Romanoff guards waited outside in the carriage.

The last picture of Max Factor during his early years in Russia, taken with his family shortly before their escape to America (L-R: Lizzie, Freda, Cecilia, Max and Davis).

One night Lizzie waited for Max with a rabbi, who would marry the couple without a license. No license, no publicity. It was not the type of wedding either Lizzie or Max had wanted, but they were together—at least for an hour each week.

As time passed, Max became more and more disenchanted. Max and Lizzie had children—Freda, Cecilia and Davis—and Max didn't want them to grow up without a father. He had led a secret life for nearly nine years, and was only allowed one day a week to see his family under less than ideal circumstances. Somehow, he had to get away. But leaving would not be easy. His fame had spread within the Court, and he and his magical beauty concoctions had become indispensable. But there had to be a way out. How? And where would he go?

His brother Nathan and Uncle Fischel had already left Russia, fearing the changes taking place. Famine had become common; religious persecution was on the upswing with the enactment of anti-Semitic legislation; border conflicts were escalating with neighboring Finland to the west and China to the east. Nathan and Fischel had settled in a city called St. Louis in America where a World's Fair was being constructed. There, they told him, Max could exhibit his hairgoods, cosmetics and perfumes.

Max hit upon an elaborate plan. He had heard about Carlsbad, a resort where ailing Court members were sent to recuperate. Using his make-up kit, he gave himself a sickly pallor and, soon, he was ordered to Carlsbad for two weeks of rest and relaxation. But he never got there. Instead, he, Lizzie and the children made their way by foot across hillsides and through woods

to the nearest seaport, careful to avoid open spaces for fear of being caught. At the sight of anyone suspicious, Max covered the children with a blanket of leaves. When the family at last reached the seaport, the steamship *Molka III* was boarding. No passports were necessary in those days, and money was not a problem. Over the years Max had amassed savings of $40,000.

Shortly after the ship departed on February 13, 1904, Max met a fellow traveler, a man who spoke several languages, including English. Max was impressed, believing that to be a success in America it was necessary to speak the language. In time, Max did learn to speak English, but he never mastered reading or writing. He could sign his name, and that was it. It would be left for his children to translate for him.

By the time *Molka III* pulled into port, and the passengers were on the ferry to Ellis Island, Max and the stranger had become partners for Max's hoped-for venture at the Fair. He also entered his new country with a new name. During processing on Ellis Island, Faktor became Factor.

The journey from New York to St. Louis took two days by train. On arriving in St. Louis, Max settled his family near Nathan and Fischel in a small rear apartment on Washington Street. Then, with the help of his new partner, he was able to secure exhibit space at the Palace of Varied Industries and Manufacture. The area was tiny, and not in the best location, but at such a late date, only days before the Fair's much-publicized opening, he felt fortunate just to be included. Max was one of 630 Russian exhibitors. Although the Imperial Russian Government had abstained from taking any official part in the Fair, its subjects were free to show their products.

The Louisiana Purchase Exposition, as the St. Louis World's Fair was also known, was a huge success, attracting nearly 20

Singers and dancers from Moscow presented their national songs and dances at the Russian Theater on the Pike at the St. Louis World's Fair.

RUSSIA

The Greatest Features ON THE PIKE

THE VERY FIRST TIME IN AMERICA

1st A Trip to Siberia
Marvelous and Realistic

2d The Imperial Russian Temple
40 Singers and Dancers Direct From Moscow

3d Russian Village and Bazaar
Composed of 75 Natives in Realistic Life Scenes

Beyond doubt the most interesting show on the Pike, and the very first time a Russian attraction has ever been exhibited at an exposition held in America.
DON'T MISS IT

According to a handbill of the day: "In spite of their sorrows at home, they present their program with brave sprightliness." Max Factor knew of the entertainers from his days serving the Russian theater.

DAILY OFFICIAL·PROGRAM

SATURDAY · SATURDAY

WORLD'S·FAIR

LOUISIANA PURCHASE EXPOSITION
ST. LOUIS, U.S.A.
1904

The St. Louis World's Fair issued a daily program that listed events taking place, along with a guide to the fairgrounds and exhibits. The Fair was open every day but Sunday during its seven-month run.

Crowds jam the walkways of the fairgrounds to view the Children of All Nations Parade. Max Factor exhibited such items as hairpieces, jeweled combs and perfumes.

Cosmetic machine used by Max Factor at the St. Louis Fair.

Few customers had the luxury of indoor plumbing, but they could take a bath in the basement of Max Factor's St. Louis barber shop for 25¢ before getting a shave and a haircut. Max Factor (right, in doorway) stands with his four-year-old son, Davis, and two employees.

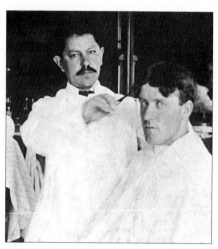

million people during its seven-month run. It seemed everyone was singing the new song "Meet Me in St. Louis," not only at the Fair but across the nation.

With the closing of the Fair began a series of tragic events for Max Factor. First, his partner disappeared, taking Max's money and all of Max's saleable goods including hairpieces, creams, combs and perfumes.

Max was devastated. Left with virtually nothing, he had to start over. Make-up had become his driving interest, but he could always fall back on cutting hair to earn a living. With initial help from his brother and uncle, he opened a barber shop on Biddle Street and the family moved into a small apartment over the shop.

Just as life began to improve—he had a new son, baby Frank

The sudden death of Lizzie Factor made the news in the Sunday morning edition of the *St. Louis Globe Democrat* on March 18, 1906. It was later learned that she died of a brain hemorrhage.

Woman Falls Dead on Sidewalk
Mrs. Lizzie Factor, wife of Max Factor of 1513 Biddle street, fell dead at Biddle and Thirteenth streets yesterday, presumably from heart disease.

(Max Jr.)—Lizzie suddenly died. When they were still in Russia, with Max so often away, his children had no father. Now their mother was gone.

It was important to Max to have his family complete again. His children needed a mother.

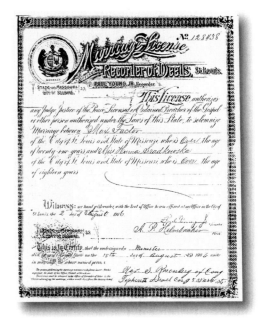

In the old country, he had known a family named Sradkowska, a wonderful family with several lovely daughters. In particular, he remembered Huma. Articulate and creative, she made dolls and delicate doll clothes and tutored wealthy children. Although she was years younger than Max, she seemed ideal. He wrote to the Sradkowskas to ask permission to marry their daughter and they consented, sending her to the United States.

The union with Huma, whom Max called Helen, seemed to work for a time. But following the birth of another son, Louis, the relationship between Max and his mail-order bride began to fall apart. Helen did not care for diapering her own baby, let alone be a mother to four others not her own. She felt Max was too old for her, berated him in front of others and would disappear for long periods without explaining her whereabouts. When living with Helen became unbearable, Max filed for divorce. Following a yearlong court battle, he was given custody of the children.

Following Lizzie's death, Max Factor married Huma (Helen) Sradkowska on August 15, 1906. With the dissolution of that marriage, he wed Jennie Cook on January 21, 1908.

A neighbor with old world charm suddenly appeared to offer assistance to Max and his family. For Max, an angel had come from heaven. Her name was Jennie Cook and the children adored her. So did Max. On January 21, 1908, Max and Jennie were married.

As Max's life began to return to normal once again, another change loomed ahead. His barber shop was making money, but cutting hair for a living had never been his dream. He had heard stories about an infant industry—motion pictures—that was beginning to take hold farther west, and he was intrigued. Perhaps his future lay in selling wigs, hairpieces and cosmetics to the actors and actresses working in these pictures, he reasoned.

If ever he was to make a move, this was the time. There may be risks, he told himself, but he was willing to take the chance.

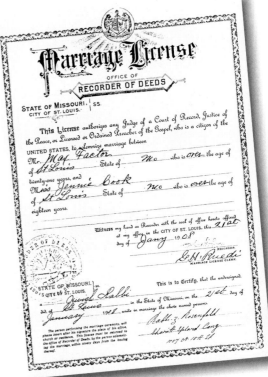

Cowboy star Tom Mix, a real cowboy and former Texas ranger who was brought to Hollywood to make Westerns, refused at first to wear make-up. He considered it "too sissy" until he saw his first appearance on screen without it.

Chapter 2

California

$\mathcal{M}$ax Factor and his family arrived in Los Angeles on October 11, 1908. Opening a tiny shop on Central Avenue in the downtown area, he started selling haircuts, hair switches and wigs. Outside, the sign read: "Max Factor's Antiseptic Hair Store. Toupees made to order. High grade work." Less than three months later, on January 2, 1909, he founded Max Factor and Company.

Ben Turpin (left), Louise Fazenda (right) and Charlie Chaplin were among the early film comedians who first discovered the advantages of Max Factor's new cinema make-up. The slapstick actors found that it did not crack on drying, as did heavy stick greasepaints, allowing them greater facial expression on screen.

The migration of moviemakers from New York, New Jersey and Chicago was moving more slowly than Max had hoped. Francis Boggs and Thomas Person, who worked for Thomas Edison's chief rival, Col. William N. Selig, had arrived several years earlier and were making films regularly. D.W. Griffith was on his way, bringing his Biograph Company and star players, including Mary Pickford, Mack Sennett, Henry Walthall and "The Biograph Girl," Florence Lawrence. There were others as well, drawn by the never-ending sunshine, open spaces and cheap land. By the end of 1911, 154 film companies had established a foothold, either in Los Angeles or its neighboring suburb of Hollywood.

Max Factor was establishing his own foothold, not only among touring theatrical players and vaudevillians but also among the growing number of performers who were coming to Los Angeles to appear in motion pictures. He had his own small line of theatrical make-up products—face powder, rouge, cleansing cream and lip rouge (applied with a brush)—which his children helped package. He was also the West Coast distributor for both Leichtner and Minor, manufacturers of the famous brands of stick greasepaint and various other theatrical items. The stage people were pleased. With them, it was either greasepaint or no make-up at all. The movie people wanted, and needed, something better.

The only available make-up foundation for movie actors had been created for the stage: greasepaint in stick form. Greasepaint was much too heavy in consistency and formed a mask when it dried. It had to be applied one-eighth inch thick, then powdered. It also cracked, creating fine lines on the actors' faces.

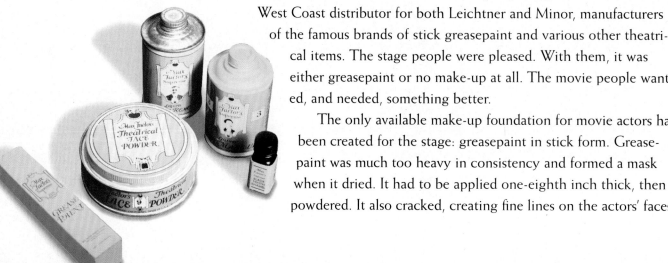

Henry B. Walthall, whose most memorable role was as the Little Colonel in 1915's *The Birth of a Nation* (above), was the first actor to wear Max Factor's new make-up specifically created for motion picture use. It was Walthall who served as the model for screen tests when the make-up was introduced.

That wasn't a problem on the stage, where audiences were seated away from the players. But on screen, especially in close-ups, it didn't work. Not only were the tints unrealistic, but unless the actors remained virtually expressionless, hairline cracks were visible. In desperation, many actors turned to their own concoctions, such as mixtures of vaseline and flour or cold cream and paprika.

Max spent countless hours in his small lab experimenting, formulating and testing theatrical make-ups in an effort to adapt them for motion picture use. He had seen as many movies of the day as possible, so he knew first hand the needs of the cinema and where ordinary theatrical make-up fell short of meeting these needs.

The breakthrough came in June of 1914 when he perfected the first make-up specifically for movies. It was a greasepaint in cream form rather than stick form and was thinner and extremely flexible on the skin. Actor Henry B. Walthall was Max's model for the screen's new make-up discovery.

It was not the dramatic actors, however, who first took advantage of Max Factor's new "flexible greasepaint." The comedians of the period—Charlie Chaplin, Roscoe "Fatty" Arbuckle, Buster Keaton, Ben Turpin, Louise Fazenda, Charlie Murry and Ford Sterling, among others—all loved it. For the comics, the new, thinner make-up finally gave them the freedom of full facial expression without the restrictions of the old make-up "mask."

Soon other screen actors were making their way to Max Factor's make-up store, including Alice Joyce, Blanche Sweet, William Farnum, Mabel Normand, Polly Moran, Richard Bennett, Marie Dressler, Geraldine Farrar, Clara Kimball Young and the Talmadge sisters (Constance and Norma).

Another breakthrough came with the arrival of Cecil B. DeMille. DeMille, who was partnered with Jesse L. Lasky and Samuel Goldfish (later Sam Goldwyn) in forming the Jesse L. Lasky Feature Play Company, had been in Arizona shooting *The Squaw Man*. Finding the locale wrong for the story, he con-

Director Cecil B. DeMille gave Max Factor his first big break in films after Factor convinced him that wigs made of wool and tobacco leaves did not appear realistic on movie screens. The agreement wasn't without a catch, however.

The release of *The Squaw Man* (1914), the first film in which actors wore wigs made from human hair, changed producers' minds about using unrealistic substitutes for hairpieces, beards and moustaches.

Mary Pickford and Mary Miles Minter were both youthful, blonde, wore long, golden curls and shared the same first name. Minter's mother was not pleased that the two young stars had so much in common. She wanted her daughter to be the standout, and she pleaded with Max Factor to do something about it. Her suggestion? Change the color of Pickford's hair from blonde to brunette. Max refused, but he was able to convince Minter's mother that her daughter would gain attention with a new, semi-adult hairstyle he had designed especially for her. It worked. Pickford kept her curls, for which she became famous, and Minter became the young sophisticate.

The young Factor boys— Frank (Max Jr.), David and Louis—appeared as Indians in hundreds of early silent Westerns so they could collect the expensive wigs worn by the actors at the end of the day's filming.

tinued westward, winding up in Hollywood where he completed the film. But not before Max Factor got to him. Max had long felt that real hair—genuine Grade-A human hair—should be used in movie wigs, not clumsy substitutes such as straw, excelsior, Spanish moss, wool or tobacco leaves. Actually, almost anything and everything could be seen on the heads, chins and upper lips of the cinema players. It was understandable in part, because the early filmmakers were usually short on money and not overly concerned with the look of the actors, particularly those seen in longshots.

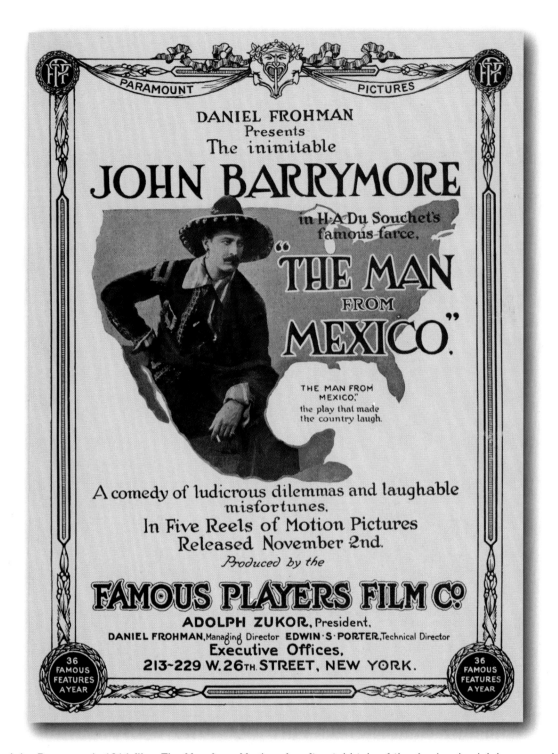

Ad for John Barrymore's 1914 film, *The Man from Mexico.* An often told tale of the day involved John, a member of the acting family known as "The Fabulous Barrymores." According to Max Factor, Jr., "One afternoon after school I was attending the front section of our make-up studio when a handsomely distinguished gentleman came in and commanded me to quickly advise my father that Mr. Barrymore wished to see him. My father was busy in his laboratory at the rear, but I did as I was told. Mr. Barrymore had a way about him that demanded service swiftly and without wasted time for idle conversation. Within seconds I was on my way to the lab to announce that Mr. Barrymore awaited. 'Which one?' my father asked, knowing that both John and Lionel had come to town to make a picture. Apparently his voice had carried to the front of the store. Before I had a chance to answer came the booming and rather impatient reply, 'Ethel!' "

DeMille wasn't interested in Max's offer, but Max was persistent, and ultimately convinced DeMille to use real hair for the wigs in *The Squaw Man*. There was a hitch, however. Max's handmade wigs were quite expensive and DeMille refused to spend the money. But he would rent the wigs.

Max had never thought about renting his hairgoods. It was an idea that presented problems. Was DeMille willing to put down a rather hefty deposit? What guarantee would Max have that the wigs would be returned in reusable condition at the end of a day's filming? Who would be responsible for the costly wigs?

The growing Max Factor family in Los Angeles, ca. 1917. (From left, standing: Max Jr., Cecilia (Celia), Freda; seated: Davis, Jennie with baby Sidney, Louis and Max.)

Now that DeMille was sold on the idea, Max could not afford to lose him. He would rent the wigs to DeMille if DeMille would use his sons—Louis, Davis and Frank (Max Jr.)—in the film's mob scenes. If the boys were part of the movie they could keep their collective eyes on the wigs while they were in use, see that none were lost or

Bebe Daniels wears Max Factor-created "Rosebud Lips," a popular lipstyle from 1917 into the 1920s.

Nita Naldi (wearing Max Factor's "Vampire Lips") and Carmel Meyers were probably more responsible than any other individuals for the quick acceptance of the new color harmony make-up by local retailers. The two stars were among the first to try it, and they were loud and unceasing in their praise. The opinions of popular performers certainly carried weight in those days, just as they do today.

Elegant, stylized cover of 1917 Max Factor brochure which tastefully avoided mention of the products it promoted: toupees for men. Inside were page after page of "before" and "after" illustrations, along with a message that stated, "Many physicians advise wearing a toupee when hair is gone since one is exposed to colds of the head, which produce catarrhal troubles, headaches, neuralgia and kindred ailments. The head is also protected against the annoyance of flies and other insects which seem to have a special liking for a bald head." The custom hairpieces were closely hand knotted and featured invisible hair lace parts and short, fine hair along the front edges to duplicate a natural hairline.

Max Factor's original Henna Shampoo for theatrical performers, ca. 1916. The product was packaged in a robin's-egg blue envelope.

damaged and collect them at the end of each day.

DeMille agreed, but the boys weren't too thrilled. It was bad enough having to rise before dawn, then be trucked miles into the Hollywood hills for location shots. It was worse having to find the wigs that were thrown to the winds as the director yelled "cut." Pick-ups, after the massacre scenes between the cowboys and Indians, were the worst. Hairpieces were buried under tumbleweeds. Others dangled from branches high in trees. Poor Frank (Max, Jr.) hated horses. But it wasn't the horse's fault he broke his arm.

The *Squaw Man* was an instant hit, proving to every producer in town that the day of clumsy substitutes for wigs, beards and moustaches was over. From then on, Max Factor's hair department had all the business it could handle.

The bonanza continued for the Factor kids, as well. Between 1913 and 1916 they appeared in hundreds of Westerns, primarily as Indians. Despite their discomfort at the time, it

Supreme Liquid Whitener for whitening the neck, shoulders, arms and hands, ca. 1918. The product was packaged in a metal can with a dusty pink wrap-around paper label showing Max Factor's image. Bold type stated: "Will not rub off. Contains no lead. Is not injurious and gives the skin a natural color."

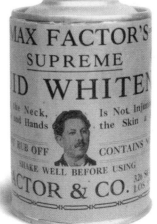

primarily as Indians. Despite their discomfort at the time, it was a job they took seriously since the cost of missing wigs was deducted from their token paychecks.

In 1916, with his business steadily increasing, Max Factor moved to somewhat larger quarters on South Broadway in downtown Los Angeles. It wasn't a big step upward, but still an improvement over the Central Avenue store. Although Max was gaining a reputation for hairgoods, his interest in make-up was stronger than ever. He now believed more distinction was necessary to classify the various shades of brown hair between blonde and brunette, which led him to coin the word "brownette." (According to Max Factor, 50% of all women were brownettes. Previously, they had been described as either "dark blonde" or "light brunette.") The new terminology would be an invaluable aid in correctly classifying women with brown hair when he later developed his revolutionary "Color Harmony" make-up line, but the term brownette would eventually fade into obscurity.

Billboard in Hollywood for Max Factor's "Supreme" brand, ca. 1918. Factor's non-theatrical "Society" line for the public was not yet available, and it wasn't until 1920 that he began referring to his beauty products as make-up, rather than cosmetics. The term eventually caught on to such an extent that his competitors were forced to use it as well.

For years, make-up in the movies had been a neglected art. The studios did not have make-up departments, so the stars who had yet to discover Max Factor were left to do their own make-up. Starting in February of 1917, however, the system began to change. For the first time, all make-up problems were considered and provided from a film's script. The procedure was directed by Max Factor for Paramount's *Joan the Woman*, starring Geraldine Farrar.

As the movies had grown, so did Max Factor's greasepaint and Indian wig business. Now a new era in films was about to begin.

Phyllis Haver broke into films in 1917 as a Mack Sennett bathing beauty, and her pretty face became the target for numerous tossed custard pies. By 1919, however, she had become a popular leading lady in dramatic films, primarily as a seductive temptress. It was for Phyllis Haver that false eyelashes were invented. Max Factor created them especially to enhance close-ups during her transition to feature films. From then on, every star wanted them. (Haver carried her make-up in the top of a ten-cent wicker basket.)

Mae Murray was the first of Hollywood's glamour girls to use Max Factor's new powder brush, introduced in 1921. The powder brush was said "to insure the ultimate complexion smoothness for motion picture players." It soon became an indispensable beautifying requisite for women throughout the world.

When Douglas
Fairbanks requested a
body make-up immune to
perspiration for his imaginative
and stunt-filled Arabian nights fantasy,
The Thief of Bagdad (1924), Max Factor
created it for him. It was also the first body
make-up that would not rub off during rigorous
athletic feats.

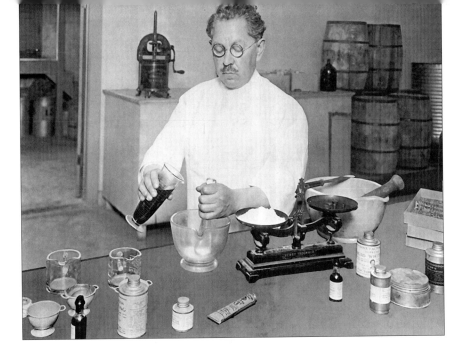

Max Factor, the chemist, at work in his basement lab on South Hill Street, 1922.

believing them to be more convenient and hygienic than the stick form, which was often messy and difficult to use.

The cool reception he had received at Leichtner, intentional or not, resulted in the launching of the world's first "sanitary" make-up. Before long, Max Factor's brand of greasepaint was outselling both Leichtner and Minor combined, making it the largest selling single brand of greasepaint on the market.

By now, Max Factor was becoming recognized as an innovator in his field. But his fame was known primarily in Los Angeles and Hollywood. That would soon change with the premiere of *The Jazz Singer* and the first national distribution of Max Factor's "Color Harmony" make-up.

> "No girl with facial blemishes or imperfections should ever let the world see them in these days of the modern cosmetic art. I could name ten stars with facial blemishes, but they never show on the screen or in public. Why? Because the stars use cosmetics so cleverly that they conceal their facial imperfections."
>
> *Max Factor (March, 1926)*

Twenty-year-old Frank Factor (Max Jr.) and technician in the well-stocked research lab above the South Hill Street store, 1924.

In the 1920s, Venice Beach was Southern California's favorite playground. Mae Murray, Janet Gaynor and Norma Shearer had nearby beach houses. Harold Lloyd and William S. Hart had cottages overlooking the canals. Douglas Fairbanks, Rudolph Valentino, Gloria Swanson and Mary Pickford made frequent trips to the coastal community. The Venice amusement pier, with its famous rides, restaurants and ballroom, attracted vast crowds of funseekers. To Max Factor, the atmosphere was much like the St. Louis World's Fair. It was an ideal setting to introduce his new line of "Society" make-up to the public.

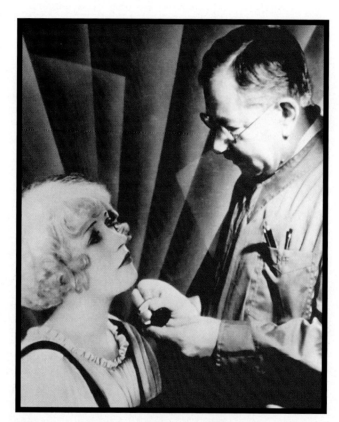

Max Factor with Marion Davies, ca. 1927. A pretty and talented comedienne, Davies was the star of Cosmopolitan Pictures, formed expressly for her by wealthy newspaper magnate William Randolph Hearst, with whom she had a legendary personal relationship. It has been said that Marion Davies might have had a more successful screen career had it not been for the overly aggressive "push" Hearst waged on her behalf, an ongoing promotion that alienated the industry and public alike.

On her arrival in Hollywood in late 1925, Swedish-born Greta Garbo was sent to Max Factor seeking "make-up dramatization" for her first American screen test. Of the early Garbo, Factor said, "She has natural eyelashes more lovely than any artificial lashes I can supply." Garbo's famous eyes captured the nation as well. Wrote one columnist shortly after her movie debut: "Until the appearance of those luscious Garbo close-ups, heavy lidded and languorous, our girls never paid great attention to their eyes save for winking and ogling purposes. And suddenly the country has discovered the paramount importance of assisting Nature with the normal eye. Even our nicest people have begun to use mascara and eye shadow. A few years ago, any woman using those devil's tricks would have been called 'fast' and cut dead by the minister's wife. Now, thanks to this seductive Scandinavian, nice women are addressing their eyes, especially for evening wear, and are still received at the parsonage."

In 1925, Max Factor received the largest single order of body make-up to date: more than 600 gallons for MGM's epic *Ben Hur*. (Above: spectators watch *Ben Hur's* famed chariot race.)

On the October evening in 1927 when Max Factor, and almost everyone else in the film industry, attended the Hollywood premiere of *The Jazz Singer,* he had no idea that "talkies" would affect the art of make-up. But he soon admitted, "how wrong I was." The initial problem was the lighting. Because the microphones used for the new sound movies picked up the sputter of the carbon lights—the standard film lighting for 15 years—tungsten lamps had to be substituted. Although the newer tungsten lights were silent, they were also hotter, and banks of them had to be used. But the light they provided was softer. The old orthochromatic film, which had been used since the birth of the industry, wasn't sensitive enough to properly record images with the new lighting. A switch was made to the more sensitive Panchromatic film. Now every item in the Max Factor make-up line for motion pictures became useless. The new film demanded a much wider range of tints, along with thinner, even more transparent applications of make-up in order to present glowing, natural-looking complexions on the screen. Right: Ad for the New York showing of *The Jazz Singer* with its star, Al Jolson (above).

ROXY, the master showman, captures the *greatest attraction* in the world for the *greatest theatre* in the world.....

...BEGINNING MARCH 24 th

L JOLSON

in

L SINGER "

ROXY THEATRE

First run in New York following the 25 week twice daily engagement at the **WARNER THEATRE**

And day and date in 234 other theatres throughout the country....

SUPREME TRIUMPH

The waterproof make-up worn by Esther Williams in her swimming scenes for MGM in the 1940s and 1950s was actually created for the silent film, *Mare Nostrum* (1925). Until the mid-1920s, regular movie make-up was not suitable for underwater activities or violent storm scenes. However, actor/director Rex Ingram (best known for his later role as the giant genie in the 1940 Technicolor production of *The Thief of Bagdad*) was planning spectacular underwater scenes for *Mare Nostrum*. The announcement sent Max Factor and his teenage son back to the lab. Ingram was concerned that a waterproof make-up could not be concocted, prompting hourly phone calls to check on the Factors' progress. Without such a make-up the film could not be completed, and expensive financial overhead was mounting as he waited. After six days and nights in the lab—the two Factors even napped there instead of going home to bed—a formula was found which totally resisted water. Ingram's film was completed and the waterproof make-up was so successful that it was used thereafter in hundreds of films involving actors and various liquids.

Even Lon Chaney bowed to Max Factor's make-up expertise.
A master of make-up himself, Chaney carried his cosmetics in
what was described at the time as "a cross between a plumber's
tool kit and a bomb case." Actually, it was an old suitcase that
contained "everything but the proverbial kitchen stove."

Clara Bow sits patiently on the running board of a car at the studio while Max Factor puts the finishing touches on her make-up.

Citation signed by film stars and film executives was presented to Max Factor by the Motion Picture Make-Up Artists Association.

Emil Jannings in old-age make-up, created by Max Factor during the great European actor's first visit to Hollywood in 1927.

Academy of Motion Picture Arts and Sciences

Recognition of Valuable Service

By resolution adopted April thirtieth nineteen twenty eight, the Academy expresses its high appreciation of the aid and cooperation rendered by

Max Factor

in contributing to the success of the

Incandescent Illumination Researches

conducted by the Academy from

January to April, nineteen twenty eight

ACADEMY OF MOTION PICTURE ARTS AND SCIENCES

FRANK WOODS
SECRETARY

DOUGLAS FAIRBANKS
PRESIDENT

FRED NIBLO
VICE PRESIDENT

Certificate presented to Max Factor on April 30, 1928 by the Academy of Motion Picture Arts and Sciences in recognition of his contribution to the success of Incandescent Illumination Research, conducted by various branches of the Academy. For the Factors, the result of the testing led to the creation of "Panchromatic Make-Up" for use with the newly developed light-and-shadow sensitive Panchromatic motion picture film. Without the new make-up it would have been impossible to take full advantage of the ultra-sensitive film and the extraordinary illumination problems it presented to filmmakers. At the awards ceremony, Max was so moved that he could only reply, "Thank you." Receiving this honor, he later admitted, was the happiest moment of his life.

Joan Crawford, one of the most popular film stars of the Flapper era, was regarded as a "ball of energy" whenever she visited the Factor salon. According to the Factors, "She was full of vitality, restlessly jumping up from the make-up chair and pacing around for a few minutes before relaxing enough for Max to complete making her up."

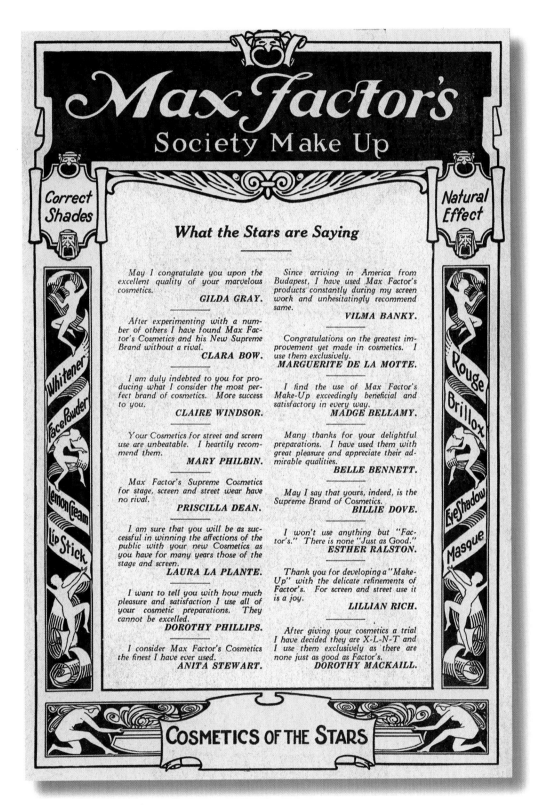

Poster, 1928.

CULVER CITY, CALIFORNIA
May 9th, 1929

Max Factor Company
Hollywood, California

My dear Mr. Factor:

In reference to your letter of recent
date, I wish to inform you that make-
ups are of vital importance to this
studio. We are constantly turning out
feature pictures and this, as you know,
requires special make-up attention.

In our talking pictures, the question of
make-up becomes even a more vital issue
than ever before, and I have found that
in using your make-up, I have always been
able to obtain the best results.

Perfect results in photography and re-
liability are the two important reasons
why we use Max Factor's Make-Up exclusively in our studio.

Trusting that you continue to keep up the
standard which you have set, we are

Very truly yours,

Frank Westmore

Director of Make-Up

Following the introduction of Max Factor's new Panchromatic make-up, George Westmore, patriarch of the family of Hollywood make-up artists and the director of MGM's Make-up Department, wrote this personal letter to Max Factor. Two of Westmore's sons, Perc and Ern, worked for Max during the late 1920s and early 1930s.

Until the arrival of Panchromatic film, blondes required the use of a special filter to soften the glare of their hair, which distracted from the photographic value of other actors who did not have such light coloring. Now that changed. The sensitivity of the new film triggered a rush of very light blondes to the screen, among them Jean Harlow, whose ultra-bleached hair had America going "platinum crazy." (Above) Julia Faye in Cecil B. DeMille's *Dynamite* (1929).

Publicity photo of Maureen O'Sullivan for Max Factor's make-up blender, early 1930s.

Chapter 4

Hollywood

Max Factor belonged in Hollywood. The stars were there. The studios were there. And, as his visionary sons kept reminding him, he had to be there.

In early 1928, Max bought a four-story building near the corner of Hollywood Boulevard and Highland Avenue. At the far corner, diagonally across the way, was the famed Hollywood Hotel. Everything about the location spelled "glamour." Everything, that is, except his new building, which had seen better days.

The newly renovated four-story Max Factor building in Hollywood housed a factory, laboratory, professional salons and an elegant salesroom.

Built in 1914, it had previously been occupied by the Hollywood Storage Company. At one time, the huge basement housed a bowling alley and a nightclub. On March 22, just 16 days after the close of escrow, a ceremony was held to dedicate the new cornerstone. A massive renovation of the entire building, from top to bottom, was on the drawing boards. Work began on April 1. Max Factor's move to Hollywood generated enormous publicity and an ongoing welcome from the community.

The grand opening was held on Saturday night, November 17, 1928. Following the ribbon-cutting, as Max walked through the front door, he remarked, "When I think of my first little shop in Los Angeles, it seems like a dream come true to enter this new building." Still reminiscing, he later commented to a reporter, "Those first screen make-ups were terrible. I realized then that a new art of make-up must be created just as a new form of entertainment was being evolved."

Max Factor welcomes guests to his new showroom during the grand opening celebration, held November 17, 1928.

The focal point of Max Factor's new Hollywood make-up studio was the great salon of Louis XIV design in green, gold and bronze. Octagonal in shape, it featured crystal chandeliers, parquet floors and mirrored panels topped by thematic friezes devoted to music, opera, dance and motion pictures. Trompe l'oeil detailing separated recessed, illuminated wall displays while prismatic glass showcases contained everything from perfumes and cosmetics to powder puffs, hairpieces and false eyelashes—all made in the upstairs plant.

Guests gather around Max Factor (center, between two youngsters) during the opening of his new facility in Hollywood. "Like the realization of a dream," he commented, "I see in this studio the greatest achievement of thought and effort devoted to the perfection of the art of make-up."

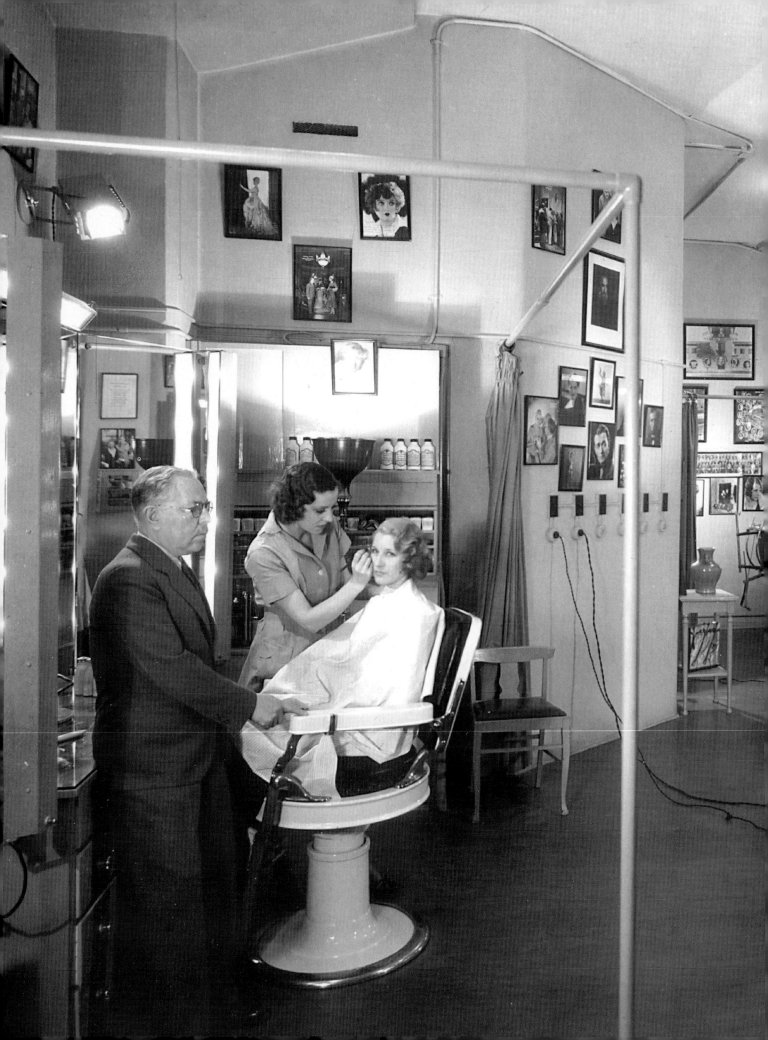

Glamorous celebrity-themed display windows became hallmarks of the new Max Factor headquarters, ca. 1919.

View of the make-up/consultation room in the new Factor building, 1929. Painted "hygienic white," it contained revolving chairs where the stage and screen stars sat before lighted mirrors that could be regulated to duplicate conditions under klieg lights, before footlights, in bright sunshine or beneath the chandeliers of a ballroom. "Light is the source of all color," said Max Factor, "and so this room is fully equipped. Any woman playing any role in life may come into it and consult experts as to proper shades of make-up that will enable her to develop the advantages of contour, color and texture—or to minimize whatever disadvantages there may be."

Actress Anita Page is greeted by Max Factor during her visit to his new salon and showroom, 1928.

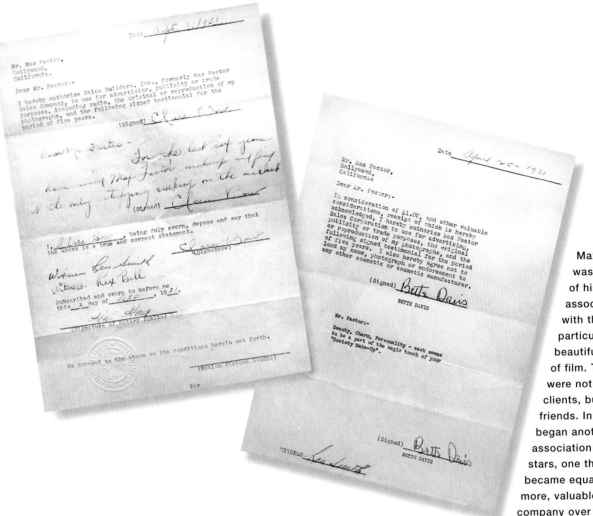

Max Factor was proud of his strong association with the stars, particularly the beautiful ladies of film. They were not only clients, but friends. In 1929, he began another association with the stars, one that became equally, if not more, valuable to his company over the years: celebrity endorsements. The arrangements were made with the stars, through their studios, to promote Max Factor make-up. In turn, Max Factor would promote the stars' latest films—all for the grand sum of one dollar. (Such an arrangement would cost millions today.) Among the first stars to team with Max Factor were Loretta Young, Joan Blondell, Clara Bow, Jean Harlow and Bette Davis. By the 1950s, virtually every major actress and aspiring starlet had signed to be a "Max Factor Girl." Above: signed contracts for Clara Bow and Bette Davis.

Max had never been a heavy advertiser. He counted on write-ups in newspapers and magazines tempting readers with his beauty secrets. Occasionally, he appeared at various outlets around town where his make-up was sold, and even spoke before women's groups, although he was never one to publicly toot his own horn. More often than not, he would send out one of his trained representatives to demonstrate his products.

Now, as his "Society Make-Up" for the general public began to get wider distribution, he became more aggressive. The stars were beginning to sign on. A testimonial from Jean Harlow or Joan Crawford, in exchange for a plug for their latest films, was worth gold.

The testimonials were the brainchild of Sales Builders, Inc., which in 1928 had been awarded an exclusive contract to handle all advertising, distribution and sales of Max Factor products throughout the United States.

Jean Harlow ad promotes *Born to be Kissed*. Prior to its release in 1934, the film's title was changed to *The Girl from Missouri*.

Max Factor finishes Loretta Young's make-up prior to a photo session.

When Richard Dix filmed *Redskin* in the Arizona desert in 1929, Max Factor took special note of the Native American Indians who had been hired to work in the production. Since Dix's role was that of an Indian, and the film was being shot in early two-color Technicolor, it was necessary to develop a make-up that would precisely match skin shades.

For a spectacular flashback to Biblical times in *Noah's Ark* (1929), Max Factor was suddenly called upon to make up over 2,000 extras before the day's shooting began. Although Max had personally trained 40-plus make-up artists to handle studio requirements, few could be called in from their assignments, especially on such short notice, and the process of doing full body make-up was a lengthy one. With little time to solve the problem, Max and son Max Jr. hit upon the idea of "mass make-up." By adding a liquid solvent to their regular make-up, they could spray the actors' bodies and faces just as car manufacturers painted their products. Spraying provided a quick solution for large groups of extras only. Stars and featured players who required close-ups still had to be carefully and individually made up.

It was one thing to create the desire in women to want to look as glamorous as their favorite movie stars. It was something else to get them to go out and buy the products. The top three executives at Sales Builders decided to pose as clerks and actually work behind the counters of various drugstores to try and determine what they could about the appeal of cosmetics to women. And, not incidentally, how best to sell Max Factor "Society Make-Up" to them.

Max wasn't quite sure that drugstores were the way to go. But the executives had solid reasons for starting there. They explained that the druggist was known in the neighborhood,

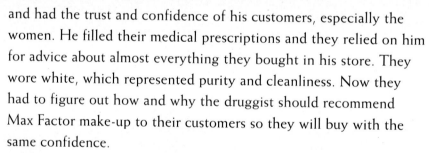

Machines fill Brillox containers in the cosmetic factory, which occupied the upper floor of the Factor building on Highland Avenue, ca. 1929. Brillox (below) added luster to hair.

and had the trust and confidence of his customers, especially the women. He filled their medical prescriptions and they relied on him for advice about almost everything they bought in his store. They wore white, which represented purity and cleanliness. Now they had to figure out how and why the druggist should recommend Max Factor make-up to their customers so they will buy with the same confidence.

The Sales Builders executives discovered that women who bought make-up usually followed a similar pattern. They purchased one brand of face powder, another of rouge, and still another of lipstick. The rather lofty ambition of Sales Builders was to sell them all three products bearing the Max Factor label.

By adapting Factor's "Color Harmony" principle to their companion selling goal, they developed the world's first "Color Harmony Prescription Make-Up Chart" and began concentrating on sales of powder, rouge and lipstick as one unit. The trick was to provide all three products in specific shades that were complementary to each other and then key them to suit every combination of complexion, hair and eye coloring.

Publicity photo of Max Factor with
Jean Harlow, applying mascara, 1931.

Drugstore window featuring display of Max Factor's new "Society" make-up line, 1929. Highlighted were cut-outs of such stars of the day as Joan Crawford, Josephine Dunn, Lina Basquette and Reneé Adoreé (shown with Max Factor in the above photo).

The last element to capture attention and interest—and perhaps the most intriguing—was the "Complexion Analysis Card." Cosmetics might have been the last thing a woman had in mind when she entered the store. But before she left, the druggist would ask her one question: "Have you ever had your complexion analyzed?" Before she could say "no" she was handed the little card, which listed the various types of complexion colorings along with colors of hair and eyes. The customer had only to quickly check off the colors that corresponded with her own and, referring to the master chart, the druggist was then able to give her the correct shades of powder, rouge and lipstick to best complement and enhance her own individual coloring. Now the woman had her own "Color Harmony Prescription Make-Up Chart" for reference the next time she needed make-up. The result was a companion sale of three products instead of one.

Max Factor and his wife, Jennie, early 1930s.

At that moment, the cosmetics industry as we know it today, was born. It was also the beginning of a make-over for Max. His Hollywood salon had become a mecca for the stars. And while it was still glamorous, he believed it was yesterday's glamour. He wanted a newer, brighter, more modern and elegant look, one that was in keeping with the latest vogue in pictures: Art Deco.

Max sought out S. Charles Lee, the famed architect known for designing over 400 of the world's most beautiful art deco movie houses. Begun in 1934, within twelve months the doors were ready to open for "Hollywood's biggest party."

Paul Muni, disappointed at the failure of his second picture, *Seven Faces* (1929), bid Max Factor a tearful goodbye before returning to New York, believing his film career was finished. He never dreamed that he would return to triumph with *Scarface* and *I Am a Fugitive From a Chain Gang* (both 1932) and other films, including *The Story of Louis Pasteur* (1936), *The Good Earth* (1937) and *Juarez* (1939).

The popular "Our Gang" series of comedy shorts had numerous cast changes during its 22-year run, starting in 1922, but Pete the dog always seemed to appear the same, thanks to Max Factor. The monocle-like black circle ringing Pete's right eye was make-up. It became so identifiable it really didn't matter which dog was playing the part.

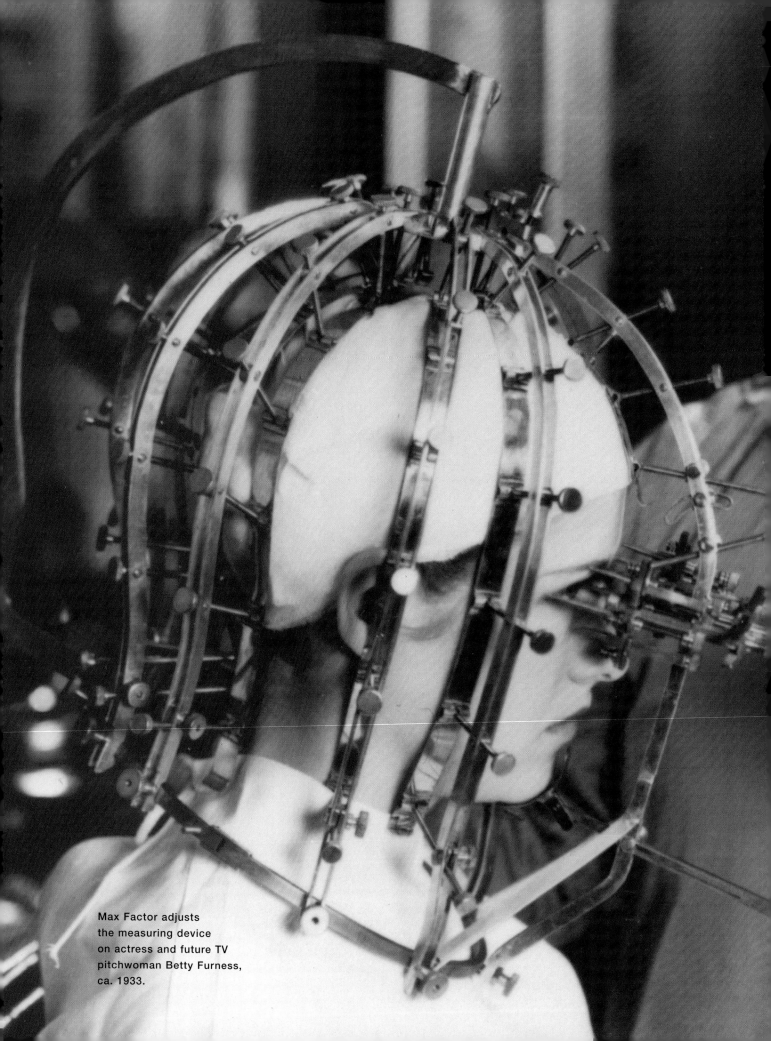

Max Factor adjusts
the measuring device
on actress and future TV
pitchwoman Betty Furness,
ca. 1933.

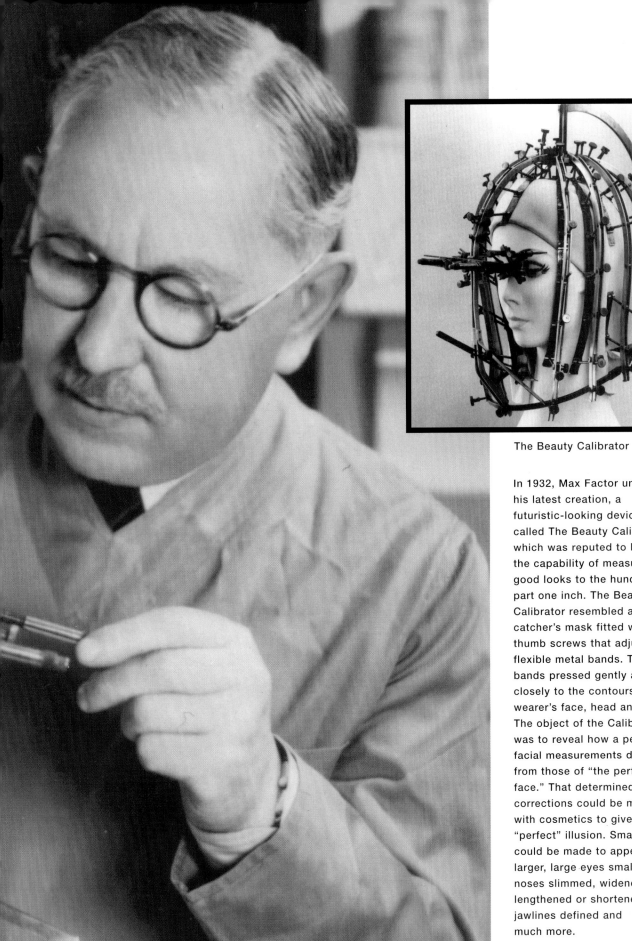

The Beauty Calibrator

In 1932, Max Factor unveiled his latest creation, a futuristic-looking device called The Beauty Calibrator, which was reputed to have the capability of measuring good looks to the hundredth part one inch. The Beauty Calibrator resembled a catcher's mask fitted with tiny thumb screws that adjusted flexible metal bands. These bands pressed gently and closely to the contours of the wearer's face, head and neck. The object of the Calibrator was to reveal how a person's facial measurements differed from those of "the perfect face." That determined, corrections could be made with cosmetics to give a "perfect" illusion. Small eyes could be made to appear larger, large eyes smaller, noses slimmed, widened, lengthened or shortened, jawlines defined and much more.

"Bee Stung Lips," the first real lip look for the movies, was created by Max Factor to solve a make-up problem. Under the hot lights of the studio, the lip pomade used at the time (lipstick had not yet been created) would run into the corners of the actresses' mouths and spread onto the greasepaint, so it became necessary to stay away from the corners. After applying the greasepaint foundation, which camouflaged the existing outline of the mouth, Max Factor simply dipped his thumb into the pomade and pressed two thumb prints onto the upper lip, then turned his thumb upside down and pressed another thumb print onto the center of the lower lip. Finally, a brush was used to delineate the lip contours. "Bee Stung Lips" (also known as "Vampire Lips" and "Rosebud Lips," depending on the role the actress was portraying) created a puckered, kissable look that was not only considered daring but highly appropriate for the flaming youth of the period.

With the coming of sound, and the creation of a new make-up to satisfy the demands of Panchromatic film, Max Factor could finally draw lips to the corners of an actress' mouth. He called the new look "Cupid's Bow Lips." (Shown on Clara Bow, right above.)

In the early 1930s, tired of playing fun-loving flappers and longing for more dramatic roles, Joan Crawford wanted to change her image. Thin lips would not do for her, she wanted big lips. Big, full and ripe. Ignoring Crawford's natural lip contours, Max Factor ran a smear of color across her upper and lower lips; it was just what she wanted. To Max, the Crawford look, which became her trademark, was always "the smear." To the public, it became known as "Hunter's Bow Lips."

Three actresses—Mae Murray, who pioneered the "Bee Stung" mouth, Clara Bow and Joan Crawford (opposite)—were often credited by Max Factor as helping to rout America's prejudice against lipstick.

Max Factor's entry in the 1932 Movieland Light Pageant, held at what was then called Olympic Stadium (now the Los Angeles Memorial Coliseum), was the "Human Jewel Box" showcasing live models and actresses. The annual event featured an electrical parade and sports festival, with proceeds going to the Motion Picture Relief Fund and the Marion Davies Foundation. New York Governor Franklin D. Roosevelt was a distinguished guest on the evening of September 29, when the stars performing were Will Rogers, Conrad Nagel, famous Western film heroes Jim Thorpe and his Indian revue, as well as a polo game between two teams of film celebrities.

Publicity still of Barbara Stanwyck applying face powder, mid-1930s.

In early 1929, soon after Jean Harlow was signed by Howard Hughes to replace Greta Nissen in the World War I aviation saga, *Hell's Angels*, the then unknown Harlow was brought to Factor with instructions to "effect an alteration in her appearance, one that would make her nationally known and talked about almost overnight." The platinum hair tint was created for the starlet, and it did open eyes. Within weeks, she became world famous, triggering a demand for platinum tresses throughout Hollywood and America. Fortunately, Max Factor was prepared for the Harlow phenomenon. A new array of make-up shades had been developed just for the young star—for both her on-screen and off-screen appearances. Now they were available for the general public as well. Until Harlow, however, none had existed.

After nearly 10 years in Boyle Heights, the Factors lived briefly in a duplex on Mansfield Avenue in Hollywood before buying a home on North Elm Drive in Beverly Hills. Other members of Max's family lived nearby. (He liked having his family close by.) Here are three interior views of the new Beverly Hills residence: the main entry staircase; dining room; and social area for entertaining, ca. 1933.

(Clockwise from top) Harlow's influence can be seen in the "platinum look" of such stars as Alice Faye, Bette Davis, Ida Lupino and Paulette Goddard during their early screen careers in the mid-1930s.

Said Max Factor upon hearing of Jean Harlow's death at age 26 in 1937: "She was simply the 20th century's most influential personality in the world of beauty. She set a style that will be copied for years to come."

Beautiful Mary Astor's long tresses, which became her trademark in films during the 1920s, were shorn in 1933 by Max Factor hair stylist Perc Westmore, under the supervision of Factor. She retained her new bobbed look for the next 30-plus years of her long career.

Left: Publicity photo of Claudette Colbert, ca. 1934, using Max Factor's powder brush.

Below: Loretta Young, wearing a light blonde Max Factor wig and Factor's "Satin Smooth" make-up, with Robert Young in a publicity still for 20th Century Pictures' *The House of Rothschild* (1934).

Publicity photo of Joan Blondell with Max Factor's manicure make-up, ca. 1934.

**Do You Know Your Color Harmony in Make-Up...
As all Hollywood Screen Stars Do?**

Not Every Blonde...
should use the same color harmony in make-up.
Not Every Brunette...
should use the same colors in rouge, powder and lipstick.
Not Every Redhead...
should risk beauty to haphazard selection of colors in cosmetics.
Not Every Brownette...
should dare to use the rouge and powder of her blonde sister.

*Excerpted from ad, 1930. (For 10 cents, the reader received
Max Factors "The New Art of Society Make-Up," a 48-page booklet
revealing the beauty secrets of the stars.)*

Architectural rendering shows proposed modernistic expansion and remodeling
of the Factor building in Hollywood, 1934.

Spacious art deco-design salon, Max Factor's new "House of Beauty," 1935.

Elegant Westfieldian marble and fluted pilasters decorate the Factor building's newly redesigned facade and addition, just prior to re-opening, 1935.

The imposing marble entrance, 1935.

Crowds flank the party entrance, waiting for the arrival of celebrities, as raspberry and chartreuse floodlights wash across the Factor building. The marquee, stretching from the door to the street, was set up just for opening night.

Chapter 5

The Party

The invitation was the size of a restaurant menu, sealed in gold cellophane and tied with a tasseled blue silk cord. It was delivered by Western Union messengers to 3,500 guests, signature required. Each invitation was individually imprinted with a different guest's name.

Invitation

The occasion was the long-anticipated opening of Max Factor's new Hollywood Make-Up Studio, and it promised to be the most glamorous event of the year. To ensure the arrival of the celebrated guests—movieland's elite—telegrams were sent on the day of the party as a reminder. Some guests received two wires, the second being from theater owner Sid Grauman, who acted as a "supermaster of ceremonies" for the evening.

At 4:00 p.m., the first surge of guests arrived, sweeping past the heavy glass doors and marble steps, flanked by bronze railings, and onto the rich burgundy carpeting. Entering the grand Salon, guests were escorted by one of the many hostesses between banks of motion picture and news cameramen to have their photos taken with Max Factor, who greeted everyone while standing on a draped platform. Then came the sign-in. Each person was asked to autograph the "Scroll of Fame," an elaborately framed sheet of parchment.

Lovely Anita Louise with May Robson, who was first to arrive at the party. (Robson's performance as Apple Annie in Frank Capra's *Lady for a Day*, released in 1933, had earned her an Oscar nomination as best actress.)

Max Factor with theater owner Sid Grauman
(Hollywood's Egyptian and Chinese Theaters)
at the Scroll of Fame. Grauman acted as
"supermaster of ceremonies" during the party.

Klieg lights criss-cross the skies above Hollywood to announce the opening of Max Factor's new make-up studio.

British-born actress Binnie Barnes (left) first came to attention in *The Private Life of Henry VIII* (1933). She arrives with fellow countryman and romantic lead Paul Cavanaugh.

Hollywood columnist Ruth Waterbury with Claudette Colbert and Max Factor.

A tour of the building followed, moving along guide ropes and red arrows through the make-up rooms, hair department, research and test laboratories (presided over by 12 chemists, all antiseptically attired), cold cream, powder and lipstick machines and rooms filled with thousands of dollars worth of perfume. Many of the guests were too astounded by the beauty of the place to even notice. As one reporter from New York noted, "They stood in open-mouthed awe until some were rudely awakened by their cigarettes burning their fingers. Then they hastily dropped them on the burgundy carpet and ground them in. In the East we use our toes, but out here they prefer to grind the lighted butts in with their heels. I think that's better. It sinks them deeper." The comment was aimed primarily at the areas surrounding the six bar set-ups. Shrewdly, they were not all open at once. As one would open, another would close, encouraging the guests to circulate.

Thirteen-year-old Judy Garland poses with Max Factor for photographers. Garland's Russian-style coat and hat were a tribute, of sorts, to Max's heritage.

Edward G. Robinson, whose portrayals of gangsters during the early 1930s made him a star, is shown a new Factor product.

Rugged leading man
Preston Foster and
party hostesses.

Young stars Barbara Pepper
(left) and Ann Rutherford with
"aristocrat of evil," Bela Lugosi.

Jack LaRue looks far from
the menacing gangster he
played in films as he chats
with a party hostess.

Leading man Phillip Holmes, the son of veteran character actor Taylor Holmes, with party hostesses.

Barbara Stanwyck pretends to add her name to the Scroll of Fame as Max Factor watches. (The quill, pen and inkwell were props.)

James Gleason, one of filmland's best-liked character actors, with his wife, Lucille.

Veteran actor Richard Tucker, who had recently appeared with Shirley Temple in *Baby Take a Bow,* with party hostess.

Silent screen star Aileen Pringle.

Esther Ralston, one of the silent screen's highest paid stars, was known as "The American Venus."

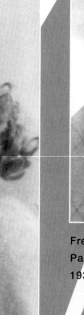

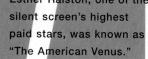

Alice White smiles for photographers. Her quick rise to stardom in the late 1920s led to comparisons with Clara Bow.

Frequent Oscar-nominee Paul Muni (He won in 1936).

Marian Marsh, whose first starring role was opposite John Barrymore in *Svengali* (1931).

Versatile character actor J. Carroll Naish.

For British actress Margot Graham, 1935 was a big year with two major films in release: *The Informer* and *The Three Musketeers*, in which she played Milady de Winter.

Superstar Jean Harlow smiles for photographers as she signs in.

Rochelle Hudson (above), a brownette favorite of Max Factor, and party hostess.

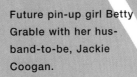

Future pin-up girl Betty Grable with her husband-to-be, Jackie Coogan.

When Hedda Hopper noticed that Louella Parsons, her rival columnist, had signed on one side of the Scroll, she signed on the other.

By evening's end, hundreds of Hollywood celebrities had passed through Max Factor's magnificent new shrine to beauty, having signed the Scroll of Fame along the way. To this day, the parchment scroll remains the most complete document of celebrity signatures from the period.

Robert Taylor and actress Irene Hervey flank Max Factor (standing on a draped platform for the picture-taking). It was at the party that Robert Taylor first met his wife-to-be, Barbara Stanwyck.

Child performer Cora Sue Collins gets a seat on Cesar Romero's lap.

It was not until nightfall, an hour or so after the doors opened, that the real glamour of Hollywood was seen. Klieg lights swept across the sky, marking the first time skylights had been used for an event other than a film premiere. The exterior walls of the new Factor building were bathed in colored lights: raspberry, gold and powder blue.

The crowds that had gathered earlier in the day to catch a glimpse of their favorite stars refused to leave until the doors finally closed at 2:00 a.m. and the last chauffeured limousine had departed. When it was finally over, more than 10,000 people had attended the party, roughly three times more than had been invited. Most of them

Edith Fellows, carrying a giveaway of Max Factor powder, chats with veteran actress Alison Skipworth, who had recently appeared in the first full-color Technicolor feature, *Becky Sharp.*

British stage actress Mona Barrie, recently arrived in Hollywood, with Max Factor and veteran comedian of "The Cohens and Kellys" fame, Charlie Murray.

Jean Harlow takes a break with her mother, Mama Jean.

remained inside throughout the evening, despite the urgings of the Mayor and fire department officials to get them to leave so others could come in. For many, the bars were the big attraction. It was Election Day and the local saloons were closed. And the drinks were free.

Engraved compact given to all guests attending the opening.

For Max Factor, whose reputation for glamour was now as widespread as many of the stars in Hollywood, the opening was a huge success. It may have cost more than most movie premieres, but it made all the papers across the country. There was no arguing, as one of the banner headlines announced: "Party in Hollywood: Even the Apostles of Overstatement were Impressed by This One."

Young Tom Brown, whose clean-cut appearance had him playing boy-next-door roles, with Marian Marsh.

Rochelle Hudson gets ready to cut the ribbon to the soft peach "For Brownettes Only" make-up room. The four make-up rooms had built-in make-up tables and three-sided mirrors, which were concealed behind sliding panels when not in use. Fully adjustable lighting made possible every type of day and night lighting condition.

Max Factor and Claudette
Colbert pause to dedicate
the dusty pink make-up
room "For Brunettes Only."

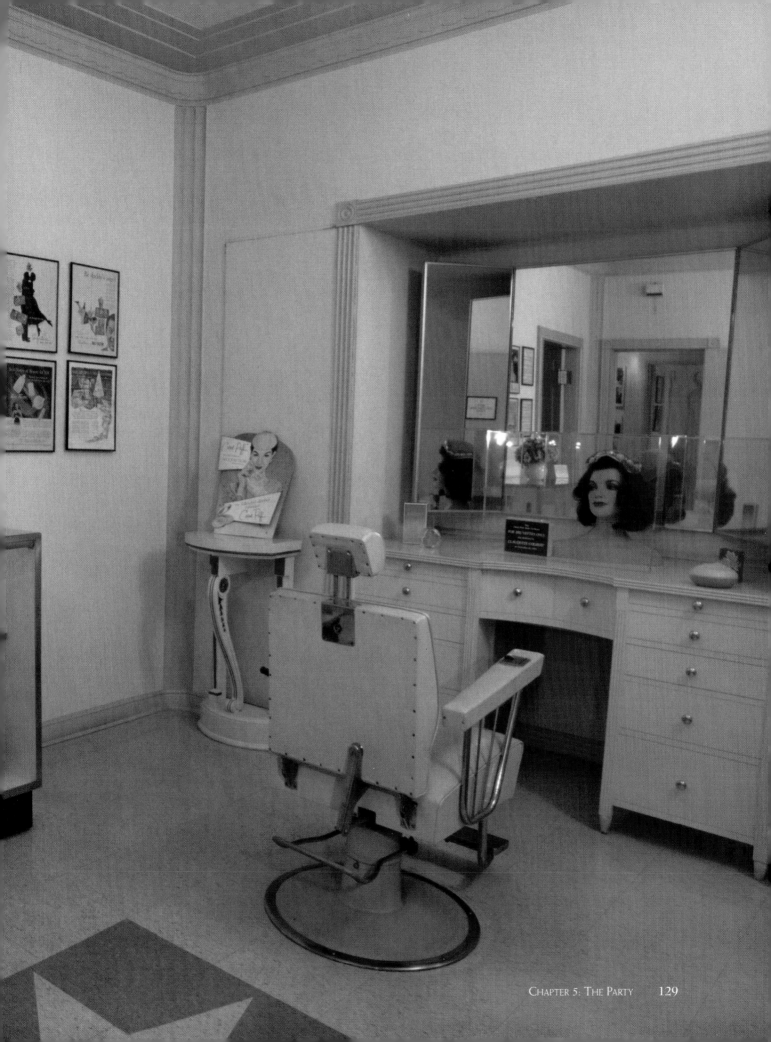

Jean Harlow poses with Max Factor before officially opening the powder blue "For Blondes Only" make-up room. Elegant furnishings— sofas, occasional chairs, tables—gave the feeling of a sitting room.

The soft green "For Red-heads Only" room was opened by Ginger Rogers, who is remembered primarily as a blonde. As columnist Hedda Hopper once commented, however, "Ginger Rogers made her hit as a redhead. Since then her hair (color) has changed as frequently as our California weather."

Claudette Colbert with her "look-alike" and those for Merle Oberon and Mae West. Other young ladies were made up to look like Greta Garbo and Loretta Young.

Young Hollywood hopefuls, including a slim, blonde Judy Garland (far right), get the glamour treatment at a make-up demonstration at Max Factor's studio, ca 1937.

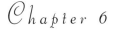

Chapter 6

Minding The Store

It was the best of times. Max Factor's new salon had become Hollywood's Versailles, its royal court, a showplace of glamour. His make-up was the standard of the industry, used by every studio in town. In 1936, a record number of orders was already flooding the hair department for such upcoming productions as The Good Earth, Naughty Marietta, Romeo and Juliet, The Garden of Allah, Mary of Scotland *and* Camille.

Robert Cummings and Marsha Hunt were the first stars to visit Max Factor's newly remodeled make-up studio following the gala opening, November 1935. They had recently met on the set of their film, *The Virginia Judge*.

And a major new project was underway: the development of a make-up for the recently perfected and much heralded three-color Technicolor process. Earlier, in 1928, Max Factor had provided make-up for two-color Technicolor, which was used in a Technicolor-produced short titled *The Viking*.

To date, only two feature films had been shot in full-color Technicolor: *Becky Sharp* (1935) and *Dancing Pirate* (1936). The color process had been lauded for its richness and sensitivity to the total color spectrum, but the performers had not fared as well, because the new Technicolor demanded ultra-strong lighting, which played havoc with actors' faces—or, rather, the old make-up. Previously, for black-and-white films, the primary goal had been to give the skin a smooth, unblemished appearance. Delicate shading normally found in good flesh tones was not required. "In black-and-white, we worked with contrasts of light and shade," said Max Factor. "In color, this is not the case. We are no longer striving for a purely artificial contrast but seeking to imitate and enhance the subject's natural coloring."

The old paste or greasepaint make-up reflected colors within a scene. Until the Technicolor camera rolled, the faces of the actors

Several weeks after "the party of the century," a call was placed to Columbia Studios for a starlet to pose for a series of publicity photos to be taken throughout the newly remodeled Factor building. The next morning, two starlets appeared. One was a slender, rather shy brunette who identified herself as Rita Cansino. The other was an attractive brownette named Rosina Lawrence. The young ladies were personally escorted by Max Factor through the laboratories, manufacturing areas and make-up rooms. It wasn't much later that Rita Cansino returned with a new look and a new name: Rita Hayworth. From then on she was a frequent visitor for make-up consultations and to pose for publicity photos.

Rita Cansino, left, and Rosina Lawrence listen as Max Factor describes various items in a lab.

appeared flawless. On film, however, their faces turned green or red or blue depending on the color of a tablecloth or chair or drapery.

Technicolor had trouble selling its new process to the studios because the stars feared appearing in color. It was better to go on suspension, they reasoned, than risk their careers in color films.

It was up to Max Factor and his son, Max Jr., to come up with a new, non-reflecting make-up as quickly as possible, one that was unlike any other form of make-up. According to the Factors, it could

Lucille Ball, who was not yet a bright redhead, seems to be saying "Me?" as she pauses outside the door to the "For Redheads Only" room with Max Factor.

Movie blood was never Hershey's chocolate syrup, as was once rumored, but it was a special substance created by Max Factor. No ordinary fluid would do. It had to flow like real blood, coagulate, be harmless if swallowed and easily washable so as not to stain costumes. Actually, Max Factor developed three different types of movie blood, two of which are shown behind the display of theatrical make-up: one for black-and-white movies, another for Technicolor and a third for two-color Cinecolor. Each could be supplied by the hundreds of gallons on five minutes' notice.

The young starlets get their first look at one of the new make-up rooms.

not contain any form of greasepaint in its composition. Once applied, it had to perform with extreme permanence, and be able to stand up without question against perspiration and every kind of activity. It could not streak, and the uniformity of color or shade had to remain without retouching for whatever period of time necessary for completion of a day's work. The make-up had to be so extremely thin that the wearer would be unconscious of it. The artist's freedom of expression could not be hampered in any way. In short, every element in the manufacture of Max Factor's Technicolor make-up had to be based upon keeping faith with Mother Nature, since the slightest touch of unreality would be immediately noticeable.

As always, Max Factor was extremely preoccupied with his busy schedule and the many demands on his time. This may explain why, when crossing Highland Avenue in front of his studio to meet a friend, he did not look up to see the approaching delivery truck. Suddenly he found himself lying in the street, surrounded by onlookers. His leg was broken, and he suffered additional incidental fractures.

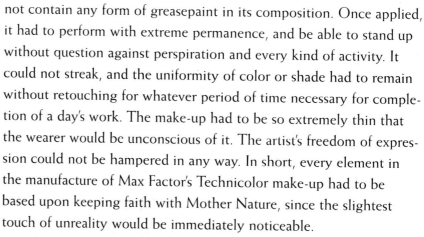

Max's family and friends rallied around him. There were phone calls and telegrams and gifts. Within the first week alone he received 43 fancy walking sticks. He kept two and sent the rest to the Veteran's Hospital in West Los Angeles.

As Max recuperated, his son continued searching for a solution to the Technicolor problem. "I was very thankful that by the time my father was able to walk again, and once more come to our studio every day, my experiments with the new make-up for Technicolor were practically finished. And with the tests showing up so satisfactorily, I was jubilantly happy when it came to showing him the results."

Carole Lombard demonstrates the Max Factor powder brush, ca. 1935.

Max Factor visits Spencer Tracy and Virginia Bruce on the set of MGM's *The Murder Man* (1935).

Katharine Hepburn wears Max Factor-created "Hunter's Bow" lips in this publicity still with Fredric March for RKO's *Mary of Scotland* (1936).

Barbara Stanwyck hears about a new shade of lipstick at the Max Factor make-up salon, 1936.

"If you have ever referred to yourself as a 'brownette,' tried a powder brush, admired a screen star's make-up, harmonized your lipstick with your hair coloring, used a lip brush, sent for a mail order wig or hairpiece, said 'make-up' instead of 'cosmetics,' then your life has been touched by the vital Factor known as Max. For all those things were invented or coined or perfected by Max Factor, who has come to symbolize beauty on and off the screen, in this country and a hundred and one others."

Helen Van Slyke for Glamour *magazine*
mid-1930s

Max Factor studies his handiwork on MGM singing star Jeanette MacDonald.

Trade ad, 1937.

Betty Grable gets a lipstick touch-up from Max Factor on the roof of the Factor building, 1937. Another Paramount starlet, Eleanore Whitney, sits next to Grable; the two had recently appeared together in *Thrill of a Lifetime*.

The new make-up was in solid cake form, to be applied with a damp sponge. For want of a better name, it was called "Pan-Cake" make-up —"pan" because of its small, flat, pan-like container, and "cake" because of the form in which it was made.

"Pan-Cake" offered a non-reflective yet transparent matte finish which ultimately was available in a wide range of color harmony tints. It was used for the first time on all cast members in Walter Wanger's *Vogues of 1938*, released in 1937, starring Warner Baxter, Joan Bennett and a dozen New York models who were billed as "the most photographed girls in the world." *Vogues* also marked Max Factor's first screen credit. "Color Harmony make-up by Max Factor" read the title frame.

"Pan-Cake" worked miracles. The film itself was mildly entertaining, but the make-up was singled out by critics for rave reviews. Wrote one: "Never before in a color motion picture have the players looked so natural and realistic. They were so lifelike, in fact, that it seemed like they would step down from the screen into the audience at any minute." Another critic centered his entire review around the new make-up.

Almost immediately, "Pan-Cake" and the New York models were used once again with equal success in Samuel Goldwyn's all-star show business musical, *The Goldwyn Follies* (1938). From then on, "Pan-Cake" became the standard make-up for all Technicolor films.

Joan Bennett agreed to star in *Vogues of 1938* when Carole Lombard refused due to her fear of color film.

My best always
to Max Factor-Hollywood
Joan Bennett

The special Technicolor make-up created for *Vogues of 1938* (1937) not only quickly and dramatically changed all concepts of professional make-up, but became the fastest selling make-up essential in the history of the cosmetic industry.

Cast and crew of *Vogues of 1938*, including the New York models hired especially for the film. When the models returned east for modeling assignments, they took with them all the "Pan-Cake" make-up they could carry, and created a sensation.

Projected images of Vera Zorina from *The Goldwyn Follies* show the make-up technician how "Pan-Cake" photographs under various Technicolor lighting conditions.

Before the release of *The Goldwyn Follies* however, a strange thing happened. As the models disappeared for their return to New York, so did all the "Pan-Cake" make-up. They had loaded up all they could carry to take back east with them, cleaning out the studio shelves. (MGM reportedly lost over $2,000 worth of "Pan-Cake" in one month.) Soon, a number of stars were requesting "that make-up in the little pan," not just for motion pictures but also for their off-screen appearances. It was only a matter of time before Max Factor would release "Pan-Cake" to the public, but rather than making it easily available, it was deliberately held back. The more difficult "Pan-Cake" was to obtain, the more the demand for it grew.

Nine months later, "Pan-Cake" by Max Factor was introduced nationally to the women of America. Launched with distinctive, full page, two-color ads in *Vogue* magazine—each featuring a screen star's portrait and an illustration of the product—"Pan-Cake" immediately became the fastest and largest selling single make-up item in the history of cosmetics, and the first of the present day fashion make-ups.

The news was not all positive. Max Factor was in failing health. A trip to Europe had been previously scheduled. The newly opened Cinecitta studio outside Rome was looking for financial backing and Max wanted to investigate the possibilities. The studio reportedly had Europe's most advanced production facilities with 16 stages and modern equipment.

Andrea Leeds played the love interest in *The Goldwyn Follies*, the second Technicolor production to use Max Factor's new "Pan-Cake" make-up.

Popular Edgar Bergen and his sidekick, Charlie McCarthy, were two of the leads in the all-star *The Goldwyn Follies*. Bergen was one of the few Hollywood personalities to admit he wore a hairpiece. Charlie wouldn't talk—not on his own—but he too had a wig block in the Factor hair department, and a spare hairpiece for emergencies.

MAX FACTOR

Supreme
PAN-CAKE
MAKE-UP

NET WT 1-3/4 OZ.

Cases of "Pan-Cake"
make-up receive a final
once-over before
shipping to retail
outlets, 1939.

The opening of Max Factor's new London salon nearly rivaled his opening in Hollywood. On the evening of February 5, 1937, 2,000 guests gathered at 16 Old Bond Street to celebrate the occasion, hosted by Merle Oberon. Highlighting the event was the then biggest transcontinental telephone broadcast in the history of both the American and British telephone companies. First to talk with Merle Oberon from London was Ginger Rogers, reached on Stage 8 at RKO studios in Hollywood. The call was then transferred to the Paramount lot where Oberon talked with Frances Dee, Joel McCrea and Ida Lupino. Next, the hook-up switched to MGM for a chat with Maureen O'Sullivan and Freddie Bartholomew, and, finally, to the Factor building in Hollywood. There, such stars as Gloria Swanson, Edward Arnold, Rochelle Hudson and Charles "Buddy" Rogers awaited. Max Factor was the last to talk with Merle Oberon and the other notables in London. Max offered his congratulations on the opening along with his regrets for being unable to attend. (Photo) Shown with Max Factor during the transatlantic phone call at the London opening are (l-r) Rochelle Hudson, Charles "Buddy" Rogers, Binnie Barnes and Eric Blore.

Promotional photo of Lucille Ball using Max Factor lip brush, ca. 1937. The lipstick brush, created by Max Factor for the movies in the early 1920s, was first made available to the general public in 1929.

Max Factor (right) attends an early "power luncheon" with film executives at a studio commissary, 1937.

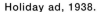

Holiday ad, 1938.

Using a cane, Max Factor visits a studio sound stage, 1937. At his side is actress Margo, who had recently finished shooting *Lost Horizon*.

Max's doctor advised against the trip, but he went anyway, accompanied by his son, Davis, and other family members. An extortion attempt during a stopover in Paris didn't help. A note had been received demanding $200 in exchange for Max's life, to be dropped off only by Max at the Eiffel Tower. The gendarmes were brought in, and a plot was devised: a stand-in, made up to look like Max, would deliver the money. The stand-in waited but the extortionist never appeared. The experience was so physically draining that Max was on the next boat to America. Once he arrived home he took to his bed, surrounded by family.

Max Factor died on August 30, 1938.

As word of Max Factor's death spread around the world, he was hailed as "Hollywood's make-up wizard" and "the man who brought the beauty secrets of the Czar's court to America." He was also the founder of one of the greatest make-up empires the world had ever known.

For all the glitz and glamour that surrounded him, Max Factor had remained a simple person. The stars called him "Pop." He was their father figure, father confessor, the sweet, kind little man who wanted only the best for them. For many, he was the reason for their success. He had turned many an ugly duckling into a raving beauty.

While his family was his heart, his make-up studio was his soul. No matter how it had expanded over the years, it was always "the store." Now everyone asked, what would become of it?

There was no question it would continue. His children had worked with him in virtually every capacity. They had grown with the business, and they knew it well. It had been said that the operation might never have progressed beyond a certain plateau had it not been for his sons and daughters.

It was the brainchild of Bill Hardwick that the name of Max Factor live on. Hardwick, who had been hired from the studios to promote the grand opening party in 1935 and remained as Publicity Director, suggested that son Frank be renamed Max Factor, Jr. The other children had concentrated more on the business aspects of the company, but Frank had followed in his father's footsteps, working very closely with him in the lab. For more than a decade they had shared experiments and tests to create any number of breakthrough products. He was the natural choice.

Max Factor and Company was nearing its 30th anniversary. "Pop" was gone, but a new Max Factor—and a family of Factors— were minding the store.

Max Factor

Max Factor, Jr.

Chapter 7

Fabulous Faces

"Pan-Cake" make-up and Technicolor were made for each other. Never before had the women of the screen looked so glamorous. Never before had their complexions appeared so flawless, so "peaches and cream." Suddenly, once rebellious actresses pleaded to appear in Technicolor.

Hedy Lamarr, Max Factor's "Girl of the Year" for 1938, was exotic and glamorous. According to Max Factor, Jr., she was the most imitated woman and, for three years, her name was the most frequently mentioned in letters received at the Factor make-up studio in Hollywood. Beginning in 1941, however, Lamarr's supremacy was challenged by letters asking for the beauty secrets of Lana Turner. Running a close second were Betty Grable and Rita Hayworth, followed by Greer Garson, Maria Montez, Merle Oberon, Rosalind Russell and Marlene Dietrich.

It didn't matter if the movie was a musical, a period drama or a swashbuckling spectacle. It didn't hurt either that the ladies were taking over the screen. The men were going off to war, to serve in the Pacific and European battlefields of World War II. A pretty face had never been needed more. Letters poured in from servicemen overseas requesting photos of their favorite stars and starlets: Betty Grable, Rita Hayworth, Lana Turner, Hedy Lamarr, Veronica Lake, Ann Sheridan and so many others—all wearing "Pan-Cake" and looking sensational. The "Pin-Up" girl was born.

Seeing the stars in color, looking so beautiful, was probably enough of an incentive for the women of America to buy "Pan-Cake" make-up. But the Factor company wasn't taking any chances. An ongoing wave of advertising appeared in magazines everywhere featuring various popular stars. In English-speaking countries a slogan—"The Make-Up for the Stars–and You"—headlined ads in print magazines and blazed across lighted billboard spectaculars. A landmark sign opposite the Palace of Fine Arts in Mexico City touted "El Maquillage Para Las Estrellas–Y Usted." The slogan became so well known there that it was later adapted to a shortened "For the Stars—and You" and, for many years, was the title of Max Factor's radio and television musical/variety show in Mexico.

Until the release of "Pan-Cake," competing cosmetic manufacturers primarily promoted creams and other skin care products for "milady." Max Factor, on the other hand, hammered away at beauty and glamour using movie stars. But with the success of "Pan-Cake" came copycat products. Practically overnight, there were 65 imitations, all called "cake make-up." It really didn't matter. The Factor product was outselling them all. In fact, the sales of Max Factor "Pan-Cake" make-up were greater than the other 65 products combined. Still, the Factors had to protect their trademarked "Pan-Cake" name from look-alike and sound-alike competition. Legal action was taken and the offending parties agreed not to infringe upon the "Pan-Cake" tradename. The largest competing product, "Pat-A-Kake," was renamed "Pat-A-Creme."

Lana Turner

To Max Factor–
Sincerely–
Lana Turner

It was ironic that cosmetic manufacturers and women everywhere had become so enamored with the "Pan-Cake" name. "Cake make-up" was a term the cosmetic industry had long and carefully avoided, having actually promised in advertising that their make-up would definitely "not cake on the skin." The great acceptance of "Pan-Cake" had forced everyone, including the Factors, to use the term in a contradictory way.

The fabulous faces seen in the movies were living testimonials to Max Factor's revolutionary new make-up. Perhaps the best thing about it, however, was that usage of the make-up was not limited to only a select few. Anyone who longed for the flawless look of their favorite movie stars could now have it for their very own.

Betty Grable signed her first agreement with Max Factor in 1938, and the relationship continued for years. Here, in a promotional photo from the early 1940s, she is seen applying face cream.

Ann Sheridan was named Max Factor's "Girl of the Year" for 1939. The vivacious redhead had become a sensation the previous year as the movies' latest "love goddess," thanks to a heavy publicity campaign by Warner Bros., which touted her as "the Oomph girl." "Oomph" was Hollywood's new term for sex appeal, replacing "It," which had been coined in the 1920s for Clara Bow. (The origin of "oomph" is believed to have been an attempt to put in writing a nasal exclamation of approval similar to "yum-yum.")

Rosalind Russell

Twenty years ago, Hollywood discovered the "vampire." The frizzy hair and the bandeau were regular vamp equipment, with a few spit curls filtering through on the forehead. The cupid's bow mouth was heavily daubed with a gooey lipstick, and the face was covered entirely with a wet greasepaint. Eyes were outlined with thick mascara.

Today the screen's "glamour girl," as conceived by Max Factor, is a much neater article. A trend toward naturalness and technical improvements in photography and lighting cause her screen make-up, lightly applied, to be almost the same as her street make-up.

News Release, 1939

The Kissing Machine

To test the indelibility of a new lipstick creation, Max Factor, Jr. asked for volunteers from the production department. An engaged couple eagerly applied for the job, but after months of testing, the young twosome began to tire of coming in early every morning. And so, in 1939, rubber molds were made of their lips and the Kissing Machine was born. This mechanical osculator had a gauge that measured up to 30 pounds of pressure. Five pounds, it was decided, equaled a little peck on the cheek. Thirty pounds was too heavy, but 10 pounds (five from him and five from her) represented a good kiss. With lipstick on her set of lips, and a tissue placed between the two pairs, the machine was set in motion. After months of testing various formulas and colors with impressive results, a new super indelible "Tru-Color" lipstick by Max Factor was ready to be introduced. (Lucille Ball was the first Hollywood actress to test that the new lip make-up was colorfast to such a degree that it would not come off in movie clinches.)

Two publicity stills of Olivia De Havilland demonstrating Max Factor beauty products, early 1940s.

Two ads featuring Lana Turner for "Pan-Cake" make-up. The early ads noted that "Pan-Cake" was "originated by Max Factor Hollywood for Technicolor pictures."

When Lena Horne came to Hollywood in 1941 to sing at the opening of a new club, a fan spotted her and contacted MGM. She soon became the first black performer to sign a long-term contract with a major studio. But the studio didn't know what to do with her. She didn't look black enough, came the word, and she didn't sing the blues. Nevertheless, just as she was scheduled for a screen test a call went out to Max Factor. In the test, Lena Horne was paired with Eddie "Rochester" Anderson for a role as a maid in *Cairo*, starring Jeanette MacDonald and Robert Young. "They wanted me to match Rochester's color, so they kept smearing dark make-up on me," Horne remembered. It was one of Factor's "Egyptian" shades, which pleased no one, especially Lena Horne. Ethel Waters got the part, and the early Hollywood career of this beautiful, enormously talented performer was never permitted to reach its potential.

Joan Fontaine, fresh from winning an Academy Award as Best Actress for her performance in *Suspicion* (1941), adds luster to her hair with Max Factor's Brillox spray. About the product, Loretta Young said, "You can give the loveliest luster to your hair with Max Factor's Brillox. Just a little bit seems to bring out all the life and sheen and actually give a new beauty to the hair."

Maria Montez, exotic star of colorful *Arabian Nights* adventure films, applies Max Factor lotion. During the 1940s, she appeared in numerous ads for Max Factor products.

Max Factor Magic...

That's what the stars call
PAN-CAKE* MAKE-UP
originated by
Max Factor Hollywood

MARIA MONTEZ
Universal Star

IN LESS THAN A MINUTE it gives you the smooth, flawless, beautiful new complexion you have always wanted.

IN LESS THAN A MINUTE it makes you look lovelier, more interesting, more exciting than you ever dreamed was possible.

Pan-Cake is another famous make-up FIRST by MAX FACTOR HOLLYWOOD. Try it today... for the beauty thrill of your life.

AT LEADING DRUG AND DEPARTMENT STORES

RKO STUDIOS INC.

780 GOWER STREET, LOS ANGELES, CALIF.

December 2nd, 1935

I hereby give permission to Max Factor
and/or Sales Builders, Inc., distributors and
advertisers of Max Factor products, to use for
advertising purposes in connection with the
matter of the advertising of Max Factor products, my name and/or actual photographs and/or
portraits of me, provided, however, that all
photographs and/or portraits of me so used shall
be obtained from or approved by RKO Studios,
Inc., and provided further that said RKO Studios,
Inc., approve each advertisement in which my name
and/or photograph and/or portrait shall appear.

The foregoing consent shall maintain until
terminated by me and/or by RKO Studios, Inc.
by four (4) months' written notice addressed to
_____ Max Factor Company _____ at
_____ Hollywood, Calif. _____
but this permission shall maintain in any event
until Dec. 2nd, 1936.

The permission herein granted and given
is non-assignable and is made expressly subject
to the approval of RKO Studios, Inc.

Lucille Ball
LUCILLE BALL

APPROVED:

RKO STUDIOS, INC.

By *Hugh Daniel*

Lucille Ball signed her first
promotional agreement with
Max Factor in 1935, and again
in 1942. Of all the stars, she
had the longest association
with the Factor company.

RKO RADIO PICTURES, INC.

780 GOWER STREET, LOS ANGELES, CALIF.

January 27, 1942

RKO RADIO PICTURES, INC. and _____ LUCILLE BALL _____
(hereinafter called "the Artist") hereby consent to, and authorize
_____ MAX FACTOR AND SALES BUILDERS, INC. _____
(hereinafter called "the Advertiser") to use the name and photograph
of the Artist for advertising purposes as hereafter more particularly
set forth, on the express condition only that credit in every case be
given RKO Radio Pictures, Inc., and its photoplay
and upon and subject to the following additional terms and conditions,
to all of which the Advertiser agrees to comply with and be bound by:

1. Such use of the name or photograph of the Artist shall be
used by the Advertiser only to advertise _____
_____ MAKEUP _____
manufactured and/or sold by the Advertiser.

2. All advertising copy, photographs, or stills intended for
use by the Advertiser, and bearing the name and/or photograph of the
Artist, shall be submitted to RKO Radio Pictures, Inc. for its written
or initialled approval prior to any use thereof, and, after approval,
shall not be in any way altered or changed.

3. Unless otherwise agreed to herein by the Artist and RKO
Radio Pictures, Inc., no advertisement whatever shall bear the
endorsement of the Artist, either expressly or by implication.

4. The wording of, and the prominence given, RKO Radio
Pictures, Inc. and the photoplay above referred to, shall be subject to
the approval of RKO Radio Pictures, Inc.

5. This consent and authorization shall continue in force until _____ 1-27-43 _____, but may be earlier terminated by RKO Radio
Pictures, Inc., upon a breach by the Advertiser of any of these
conditions.

(For _Additional Provisions_, if any, see Rider attached and
initialled).

AGREED TO:

RKO RADIO PICTURES, INC.

By _____
(Type in name of Advertiser)

By _____
(Signature)

Lucille Ball
(Signature of Artist)

No order or agreement shall be binding on this Corporation, unless in writing and signed by an officer.

"Tru-Color" lipstick was first introduced in February, 1940. The new lipstick was indelible, non-irritating to the lips and did not change color after application. Indelible lipsticks had appeared on the market prior to "Tru-Color," but in many cases the indelible ingredient irritated the skin of the user and the pigments radically changed in color shortly after application. (Above) Madeleine Carroll applying Max Factor's new "Tru-Color" lipstick.

Frances Dee applies eyeliner by Max Factor.

Ad for "Tru-Color" lipstick featuring Ella Raines, 1945.

Beautiful, redheaded Maureen O'Hara promoted Max Factor's "Color Harmony" make-up.

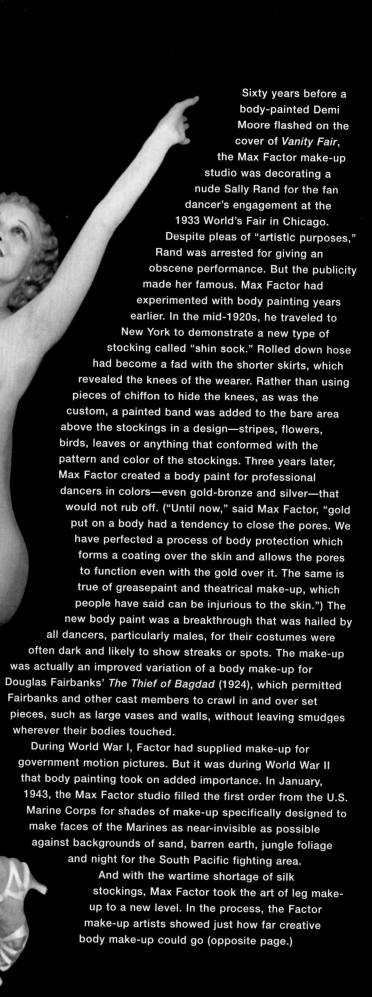

Sixty years before a body-painted Demi Moore flashed on the cover of *Vanity Fair*, the Max Factor make-up studio was decorating a nude Sally Rand for the fan dancer's engagement at the 1933 World's Fair in Chicago. Despite pleas of "artistic purposes," Rand was arrested for giving an obscene performance. But the publicity made her famous. Max Factor had experimented with body painting years earlier. In the mid-1920s, he traveled to New York to demonstrate a new type of stocking called "shin sock." Rolled down hose had become a fad with the shorter skirts, which revealed the knees of the wearer. Rather than using pieces of chiffon to hide the knees, as was the custom, a painted band was added to the bare area above the stockings in a design—stripes, flowers, birds, leaves or anything that conformed with the pattern and color of the stockings. Three years later, Max Factor created a body paint for professional dancers in colors—even gold-bronze and silver—that would not rub off. ("Until now," said Max Factor, "gold put on a body had a tendency to close the pores. We have perfected a process of body protection which forms a coating over the skin and allows the pores to function even with the gold over it. The same is true of greasepaint and theatrical make-up, which people have said can be injurious to the skin.") The new body paint was a breakthrough that was hailed by all dancers, particularly males, for their costumes were often dark and likely to show streaks or spots. The make-up was actually an improved variation of a body make-up for Douglas Fairbanks' *The Thief of Bagdad* (1924), which permitted Fairbanks and other cast members to crawl in and over set pieces, such as large vases and walls, without leaving smudges wherever their bodies touched.

During World War I, Factor had supplied make-up for government motion pictures. But it was during World War II that body painting took on added importance. In January, 1943, the Max Factor studio filled the first order from the U.S. Marine Corps for shades of make-up specifically designed to make faces of the Marines as near-invisible as possible against backgrounds of sand, barren earth, jungle foliage and night for the South Pacific fighting area.

And with the wartime shortage of silk stockings, Max Factor took the art of leg make-up to a new level. In the process, the Factor make-up artists showed just how far creative body make-up could go (opposite page.)

1943 ad featuring World War II favorite, Veronica Lake.

Ann Miller applies "Pan-Cake" make-up as Max Factor, Jr. looks on.

Multi-talented June Havoc is
shown rouge colors by a
make-up consultant.

Hal King, Max Factor's chief make-up artist, was the "cosmetic beautifier" to the stars during Hollywood's Golden Age. Shown here with a model, he later became closely associated with Lucille Ball.

Publicity shot of Loretta Young with Max Factor make-up, ca. 1945.

Angela Lansbury, having just appeared opposite Judy Garland in *The Harvey Girls* (1946), demonstrates Max Factor rouge.

For MGM's opulent production of *Marie Antoinette* (1938), the Factor hair department supplied 903 classic wigs made of pure white human hair. (Most white wigs, before and after *Marie Antoinette*, were made of Angora or refined yak.) In addition, the film required 1,200 lesser wigs, mainly for the use of "peasant" extras. Looking back on his 60 years at MGM, noted hairstylist Sydney Guilaroff called *Marie Antoinette* his "favorite picture." Norma Shearer as the 18th Century French queen, wears one of her 28 wig changes for the role. The average cost of each of Shearer's wigs was $385.00.

Chapter 8

Creating Illusions

*I*n 1945, a noted national magazine devoted five pages to the Max Factor hair department. It was the first behind-the-scenes peek into this fascinating segment of the Factor operation. Although many people had been aware of the Factors' involvement with hairgoods, the success of their make-up products had pushed the hair department into the background. It was no background business, however. In itself, the Factor hair department was a massive operation. They were, in fact, the primary supplier of hair-goods for the motion picture industry.

Hundreds of wig blocks line the shelves, each individually molded to conform with the exact size and shape of a star's head. On the top shelf can be seen the wig blocks for (l-r) Margot Grahame, Lionel Barrymore, Binnie Barnes, Frank Morgan, Barbara Stanwyck and Paul Muni.

The processing room, where the largest stock of human hair in America was stored in every type, color and length. Employees called "mixers" blended strands of different-colored hair until they formed the right tint. (It is seldom that a coal-black head does not contain at least a few strands of red. And there is no such thing as gray hair. The gray is an "intermixture" of black or brown and white strands.)

In one way or another, Max Factor had always been involved with hair, whether he was learning wigmaking as a youngster, giving haircuts in St. Louis or providing hairpieces for gents during his earliest days in Los Angeles. The real hair Indian wigs he rented out for *The Squaw Man* in 1913 were only the beginning. From then on he was the hair man to the movies, custom tailor to filmland's pates and jowls.

The phenomenal growth of the wig department during the 1920s led Max Factor to hire Perc and Ern Westmore, sons of George Westmore, director of MGM's Make-Up Department. For years, toupees and wigs made by Max Factor featured bases constructed of hair lace, an almost invisible silky wig of human hair, rather than a thread base. The advantage of hair lace was a natural-looking wig parting. It was the Westmores who came up with the idea to use hair lace for hairlines as well. Attached to the forehead and sides with

Max Factor used only pure virgin hair, hair that had never been touched by hair coloring or any kind of permanent waving. It was almost impossible to find virgin hair in America so he only bought from Europe. The best places, he found, were small towns far from the cities. Some areas were so remote that the women were paid in pots and pans, or other needed household goods, as money had no value to them. The lighter the hair, and the finer its texture, the more valuable it was. Long, pure white hair was the most costly, followed by gleaming red hair.

"Ventilators" sit in individual compartments weaving and tying hair into wig bases.

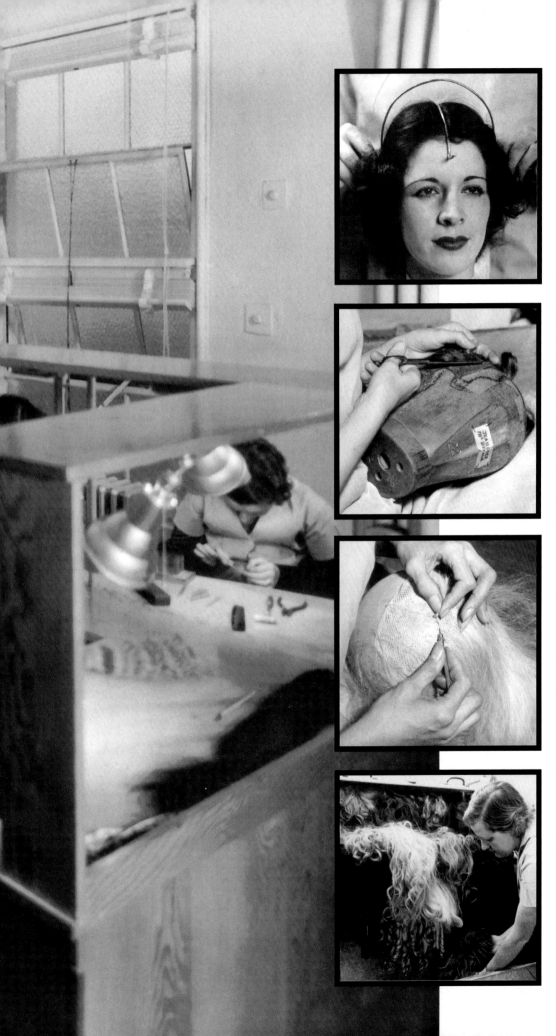

(Top) Measuring the contours of the head was the first step to ensure a perfect-fitting wig.

(Second from top) Preparing a new hairpiece for Jeanette MacDonald, using her wig block. The singing star, who achieved great popularity teamed with Nelson Eddy, was said to be a difficult customer. "Nobody told her how she should look," remembered a 35-year veteran of the hair department. "She always had to have things her way."

(Middle) In making a wig, each hair is woven or tied to a wig base. Such weaving is called "ventilating," and those who have mastered the art are called "ventilators." During the height of the Factor hair department, there were probably no more than 100 ventilators in the United States, and most of them worked for Max Factor. The wigmakers who handled white hair, as above, often had to wear sunglasses to prevent temporary "snow blindness."

(Bottom) The chemical bath, where all wigs were cleaned and sterilized.

Helen Hayes, wearing a
marcelled Percern wig from
Max Factor, ca. 1933.

Fred Frederick, head of Max Factor's hair department, sits in his combination office/research room among rare volumes and scrapbooks. The Frederick library contained the most extensive collection of pictured heads and hairdos of all nations and periods in the country, perhaps in the world.

spirit gum, it virtually became part of the wearer's skin, and was undetectable once covered with make-up and powder. The new wigs, called Percern—a coupling of Perc and Ern—generated enormous interest and business.

The Westmores remained with Max Factor until 1935, when they went on to illustrious careers of their own as head make-up artists—Perc at Warner Bros. and Ern at 20th Century Fox—in addition to founding the House of Westmore, a Hollywood beauty salon. The patent for Percern wigs was sold to Max Factor for one dollar and a percentage of the rentals of all wigs made for a number of years. With the departure of the Westmores, the Percern name was dropped in favor of "Max Factor Hairlace Wigs," a term Factor had used earlier.

Fred Frederick (left), prepares actress Peggy Wood for her role in *Jalna* (1935) as Max Factor looks on.

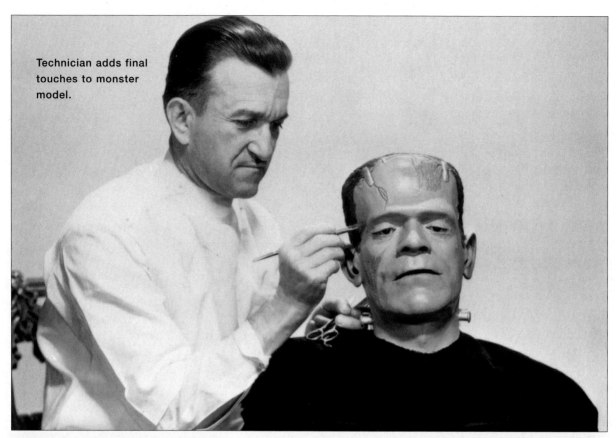

Technician adds final touches to monster model.

Pauline Eells, chief ventilator, works on Boris Karloff's "monster" wig.

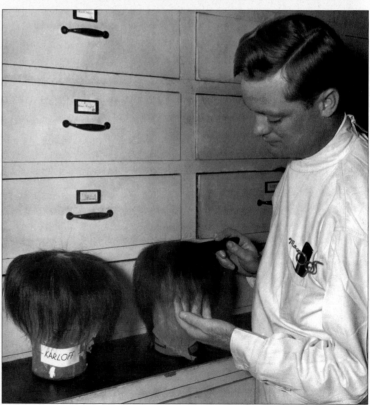

Trimming the "monster" wig.

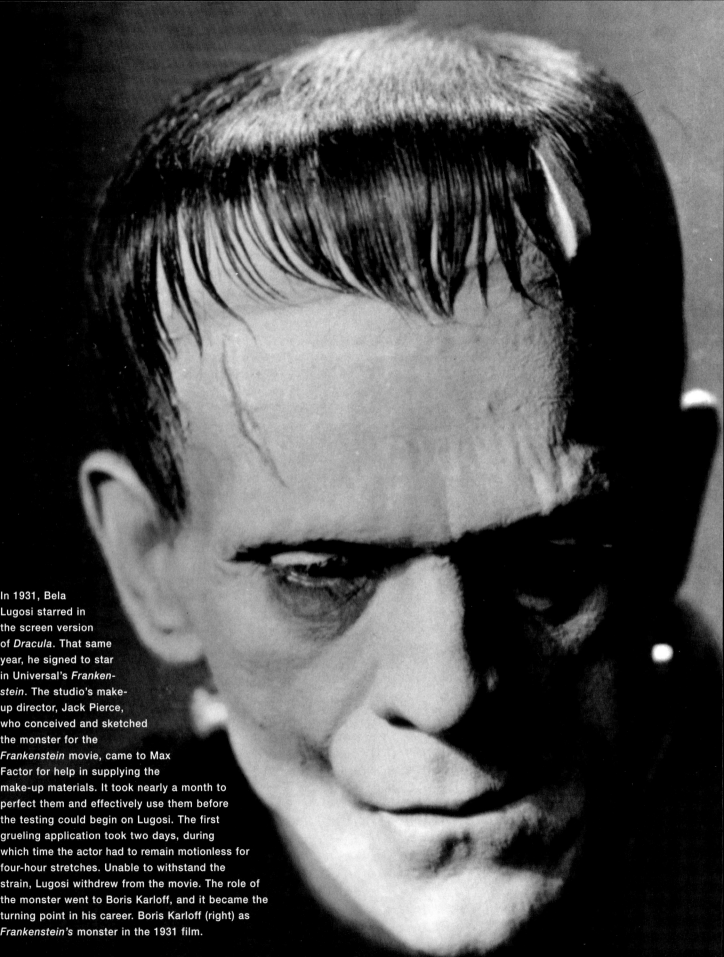

In 1931, Bela Lugosi starred in the screen version of *Dracula*. That same year, he signed to star in Universal's *Frankenstein*. The studio's make-up director, Jack Pierce, who conceived and sketched the monster for the *Frankenstein* movie, came to Max Factor for help in supplying the make-up materials. It took nearly a month to perfect them and effectively use them before the testing could begin on Lugosi. The first grueling application took two days, during which time the actor had to remain motionless for four-hour stretches. Unable to withstand the strain, Lugosi withdrew from the movie. The role of the monster went to Boris Karloff, and it became the turning point in his career. Boris Karloff (right) as *Frankenstein's* monster in the 1931 film.

Dolores Del Rio, one of the screen's great beauties, as she appeared in Warner Bros. *Madam Du Barry*, wearing a Percern hairpiece, 1934.

Fred Frederick had eagerly awaited the Westmores' move. A former wigmaker's apprentice, he had come to Los Angeles from New York in 1929 solely to work for Max Factor. "It wasn't possible then because of the Westmores being there," he remembered, "so to kill time I ran a beauty shop, giving perms." Six years later, he was hired by Max Firestein, vice-president in charge of the wig department (Firestein was Max Factor's son-in-law, married to his daughter Cecilia.)

Frederick made good in storybook fashion, supervising the Max Factor hair department for nearly four decades. During that time it emerged as the largest producer of its kind in the world. Although Frederick lost out to the Westmores in the creation of a "suit of hair" for *King Kong* (1933) he did receive his share of odd requests. There were hair pants for monkeys and a whiskered mane for the Cowardly Lion in *The Wizard of Oz* (1939). There were wigs for various characters throughout every period in history, and letters from fans wanting snips of the glued-on chin whiskers worn by Brian Aherne in *Juarez* (1939). And there were constant pleas for hair from Errol Flynn's head, real or not.

The disclosure by Frederick in 1940 that 27 of Hollywood's most popular leading men depended on Factors for hair help had women taking their men firmly in hand and either bringing them in or persuading them to write to the company. "Thousands of males interested in making a better appearance now think of us just as they do of their tailor or dentist," said Frederick at the time.

When asked if his hair was real, John Wayne would reply, "Sure, it's just not *my* real hair."

Two images of 24-year-old Robert Taylor: as a young man and aged by Max Factor, 1935. Taylor's aging was based on a mathematically precise chart developed by Max Factor, Jr., and was used as a guide for actors whose roles required them to grow older on screen. The more mature Taylor is wearing a wig.

Suddenly, men were no longer shy about wearing a hairpiece. The clientele included everyone from truck drivers and doctors to admirals. For their protection, however, a special door was opened at the side of the building which allowed them to enter without notice.

Spirit gum used to adhere wigs, toupees and facial hair.

But not all hairpieces were used to conceal an absence of hair or key a period in history. A female star may have been called upon to wear five or six different hairstyles during a day's shooting, and it was more economical for her to slip on a Factor wig than to spend considerable time with her hairdresser or under a drier. And, for both women and men, it was easier to match scenes when the actor was wearing a wig.

As big as Factor's movie wig business became, and it was on a par with the make-up department, the non-professional adjunct grew even larger. That is, until the end of World War II when, except for returning servicemen, Fred Frederick had to cut back. Said Frederick, "We have all we can handle right now taking care of the young men in the Army and Navy between the ages of 20 and 25 who went into the service with good crops of hair and started to lose it in bunches. Most of them come here because they are about to go home to see their wives or sweethearts, and they want desperately to look just as they did when they left."

The Factor hair department remained open until 1973 when it was phased out due to the introduction of less expensive, over-the-counter synthetic wigs. With the closing, many of the famous celebrity wigs and hairpieces seen in movies of the past disappeared. Those that were saved later went on display at the Max Factor Museum.

Perhaps it was a holdover from his poor European childhood. Perhaps it was the expense of natural hair, particularly the pure white and red. Whatever, Max Factor was concerned about the amount of loose hair he would find on the floor during his frequent visits to the hair department. One day he said to Fred Frederick, "You must talk to your people about all the wasted loose hair. After all, we can reuse it." As he turned to leave, he added quickly, "And tell them to stop wasting pins, too." The pins were not an expensive item but thousands were used in the dressing and styling of wigs and hairpieces.

Later, when Max returned to the hair department, he was pleased to see very little hair on the floor. Pins were still scattered everywhere, however. Without saying a word, he found a bowl and began to pick up pins. He stayed long enough only to retrieve a few, but he returned several times that day to repeat the procedure. After that, the floor remained not only hair-free but pin-free.

Edward G. Robinson, made up with wig and moustache for his starring role in *A Dispatch from Reuters* (1940). Max Factor noted that Robinson had Hollywood's heaviest and darkest beard, while Clark Gable had the toughest.

For the title role in *Cardinal Richelieu* (1935), George Arliss' look was meticulously researched and based on paintings of the period.

Dean Jagger's camera test wearing a Factor hairlace wig for the title role in *Brigham Young* (1940).

Heather Angel and Henry Willcoxon in character wigs for *The Last of the Mohicans* (1936).

Dorothy Lamour first achieved popularity in a series of South Sea Island adventures, starting with *The Jungle Princess* (1936). Her trademarks were an exotic sarong (designed by Edith Head) and her long, flowing hair (created by Max Factor's hair department).

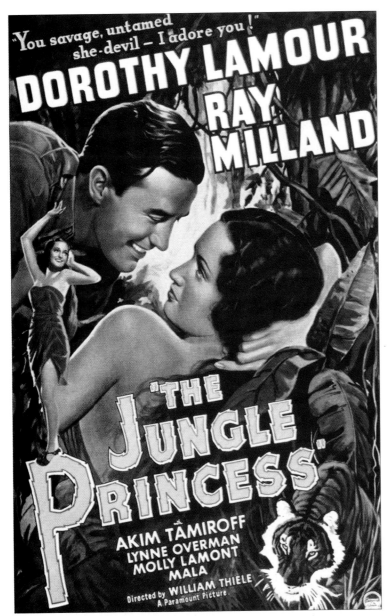

"The higher 'Mr. Monkey' climbs, the more he exposes his behind" became a motto in Hollywood during the 1930s, especially with the success of the Tarzan films and Dorothy Lamour's island epics. But it wasn't only the monkeys' behinds that concerned filmland's censors and had producers calling Max Factor for help. For potentially revealing scenes, hair panties were designed by the wig department. That didn't work either, since the animals kept pulling them off. Finally, Max hit upon a more sensible solution. "Use females," he suggested. They did, and it worked.

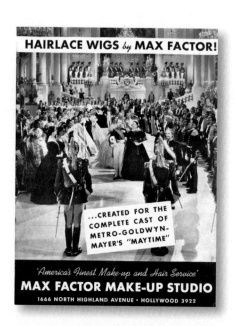

Trade ad, 1937.

Trade ad, 1936.

Preparing Chinese wigs for MGM's sprawling production, *The Good Earth* (1937). Until this film, actors were forced to shave their heads for bald-headed character roles. With *The Good Earth*, a skull cap of "artificial flesh" was used, drawn tightly over the real hair. Paul Muni was the first to wear the new cap.

Ona Munson, as Belle Watling in *Gone with the Wind*, is shown wearing her character's wig.

Wig proposal for Gone with the Wind (1939).

PICTURE Nº 108
WARDROBE STILL
ME ONA MUNS
AR. BELL
ANGE MAKE

CABLE: "FACTO"
Acme, Private and
All Standard Codes

MAX FACTOR & CO.
1666 North Highland Avenue • Highland at Hollywood Boulevard

Phone HOllywood 3932 • HOLLYWOOD, CALIFORNIA

ADDRESS ALL CORRESPONDENCE
TO THE FIRM—
NOT TO INDIVIDUALS

EXECUTIVE
OFFICES

January 16, 1939

Selznick Productions, Inc.
Culver City, California

Gentlemen:

We are pleased to submit the following proposal for your production, "GONE WITH THE WIND."

RENTAL STOCK WIGS AND HAIRGOODS

AMOUNT	TYPE OF WIGS OR HAIRGOODS	RENTAL EACH WIG AND ITEM				5th WEEK	6th WEEK	Remaining 6 WKS.	Grace 4 WKS.	Total Rental
		1st WEEK	2nd WEEK	3rd WEEK	4th WEEK					
25	Women's Wigs, Single Hairlace, Ventilated	7.50	3.75	3.75	3.75	3.75	3.75	7.50	----	843.75
25	Women's Wigs, Single Hairlace, Weft Back	5.00	2.50	2.50	2.50	2.50	2.50	5.00	----	562.50
12	Men's Character Wigs, Single Hairlace, Ventilated	7.50	3.75	3.75	3.75	3.75	3.75	7.50	----	405.00
25	Ladies' Falls	3.00	1.50	1.50	1.50	1.50	1.50	3.00	----	337.50
5	Men's Falls, Temple to Temple, Hairlace Ventilated	5.00	2.50	2.50	2.50	2.50	2.50	5.00	----	112.50
5	Men's Falls, Hairlace Neck Sides	2.00	1.00	1.00	1.00	1.00	1.00	2.00	----	45.00
100	Sets Curls	.50	.25	.25	.25	.25	.25	.50	----	225.00
200	Switches - 3 Stems Each	1.00	.50	.50	.50	.50	.50	1.00	----	900.00
									TOTAL RENTAL	3431.25

Frederic's charge total 3200.00   *charge 3431.25*

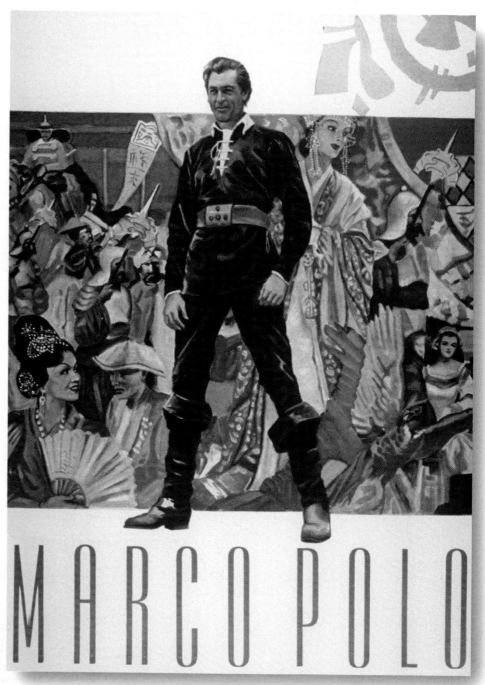

Prior to preparing hairstyles for Gary Cooper in *The Adventures of Marco Polo*, the Factor wig department received preliminary sketches of Cooper as the title character (below).

Trade ad, *The Adventures of Marco Polo*, 1938.

KUBLAI KHAN

LADY OF RANK

Sketches for wigs and facial hair proposed for various supporting roles in Samuel Goldwyn's lavish production, *The Adventures of Marco Polo*.

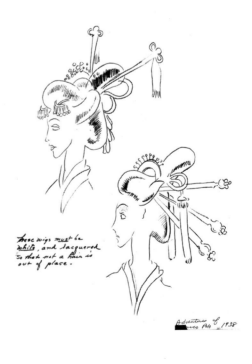

These wigs must be *white*, and lacquered so that not a hair is out of place.

Adventures of Marco Polo 1938

Marlene Dietrich demanded that Max Factor sprinkle real gold dust into her wigs to add glitter to her tresses during filming. The glamour trick was expensive. In powdered form, gold cost about $60 an ounce, and approximately half an ounce was required to add shimmer to a wig. Of this amount, up to $23 worth could be reclaimed following a day's use. The first step was to comb as much of the gold dust from the hair as possible. Following that, the hair was "placer mined" with shampoo, which finally settled the gold at the bottom of the soap solution. The shimmering images in *Shanghai Express* (1932), particularly of Marlene Dietrich, won Lee Garmes one of the earliest Academy Awards for cinematography.

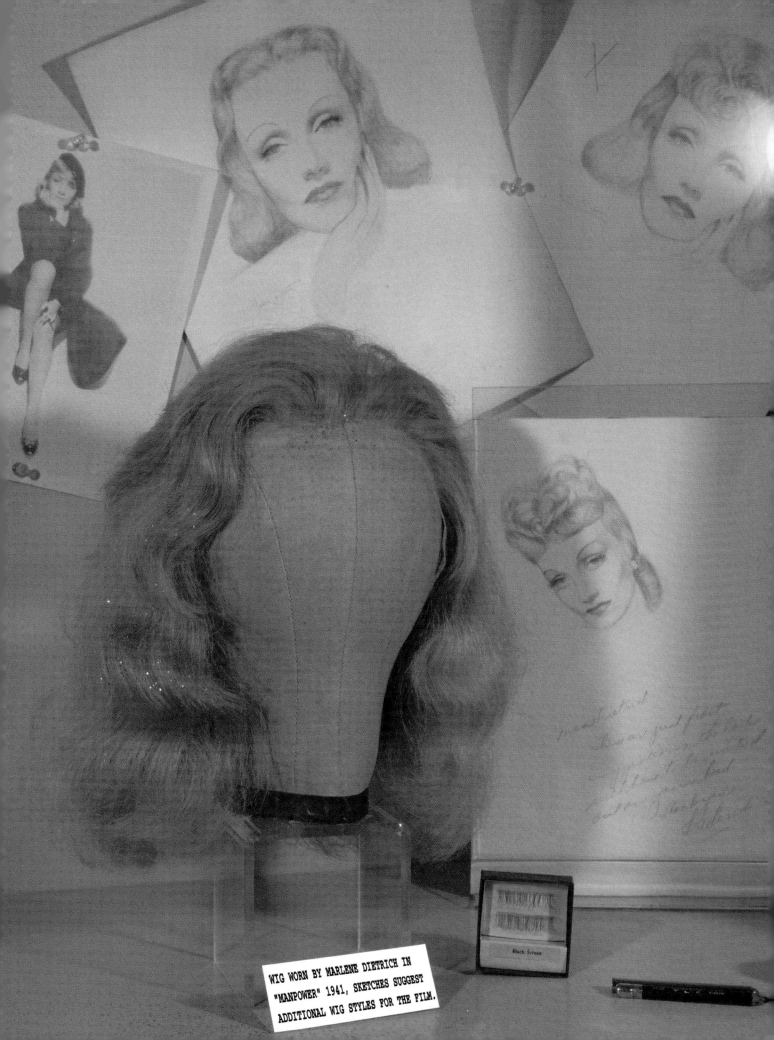

WIG WORN BY MARLENE DIETRICH IN
"MANPOWER" 1941, SKETCHES SUGGEST
ADDITIONAL WIG STYLES FOR THE FILM.

Two wig shots from *The Private Lives of Elizabeth* (1939) show Donald Crisp and Olivia De Havilland.

Signed photo of Russian-born actor Akim Tamiroff to Fred Frederick reads: "To my friend Freddy, whose great activity enables me to bring to life all the different characterizations I'm trying to create." Tamiroff was twice nominated for an Academy Award.

Jose Ferrer in make-up for the title role in *Cyrano de Bergerac* (1950) wears a Max Factor wig, moustache and goatee.

Helen Carpenter's original sketches of hairstyles for Bette Davis and Miriam Hopkins in *The Old Maid* (1939) are shown brought to life by the Max Factor hair department.

Raymond Massey refused to wear the wig Fred Frederick had created for him in *Abe Lincoln in Illinois* (1940). "He hit the ceiling when he saw that wig," Frederick said. "Mr. Massey prided himself on his knowledge of Lincolniana and, according to him, we had parted it on the wrong side. What he didn't know was that at a certain point in Lincoln's life, he stopped parting his hair on one side of his head and began to part it on the other. Why, nobody knows." Frederick had photos to prove his point to Massey, who also wore a Factor-created "Lincoln mole," complete with hairs growing from it, in the film.

Joan Bennett wears two different wig styles for *The Man in the Iron Mask* (1944).

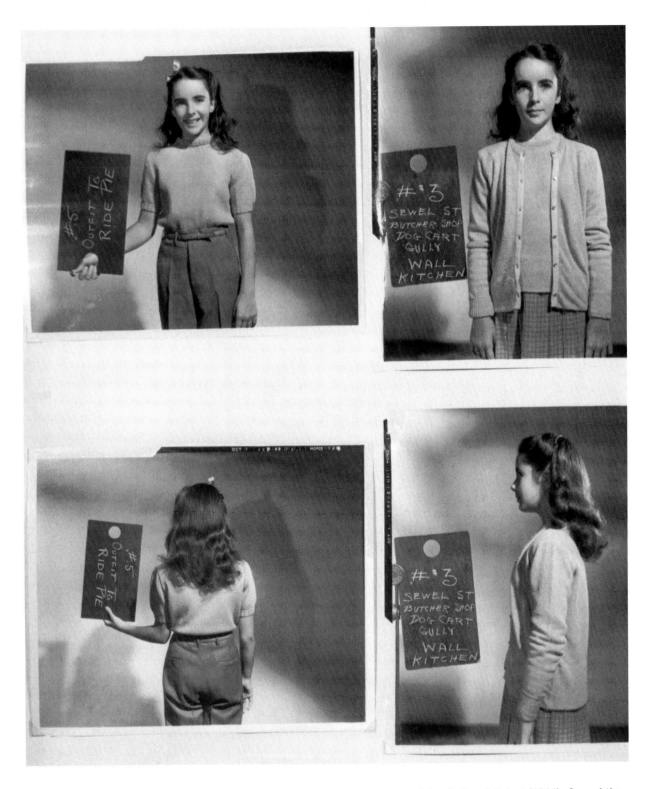

Four views of 12-year-old Elizabeth Taylor posing with a hairpiece created for *National Velvet* (1944). One of the most dramatic scenes in the movie had Mickey Rooney cutting Taylor's long tresses with blunt scissors so she could ride her horse in the famed Grand National Steeplechase. Few people realized that the hair was not Taylor's, but a Max Factor wig.

Five different wig styles for Martha Scott's role depicting the life of a small town schoolmistress in *Cheers for Miss Bishop* (1941).

To demonstrate the versatility of the Factor hair department in 1942, a one-reel film was produced titled *The Magic of Make-Up*. In the film, a then-unknown actor named Robert Mitchum had his chest shaved. The hair was then replaced with a realistic rug of chest hair created by the Factor hair technicians.

Publicity still showing Linda Darnell wearing a Max Factor wig created for *Forever Amber*.

Marquee of New York's Roxy Theater, 1947.

Fred Frederick works on a wig for Cornel Wilde's character in *Forever Amber* (1947). The Max Factor hair department turned out 4,402 wigs for the period drama, based on Kathleen Winsor's bestselling novel. It was the largest wig order of all time.

Two of many wig changes given Rosalind Russell for her eccentric title character in *Auntie Mame* (1958).

Ingrid Bergman didn't want to have her hair cut. Fred Frederick didn't want to cut it. But Bergman's role in *Joan of Arc* (1948) demanded a drastic trim. The result was the "Bergman Bob." Even before the release of the film, other Hollywood stars were sacrificing their long tresses in favor of the new Bergman cut, feeling that it was the right look to go with the "New Look," the hot fashion style of the day. (The "New Look," created by Christian Dior, was typified by rounded shoulders, full bust, nipped waist, padded hips and long, sweeping skirts supported by petticoats and high heels.) Soon the "Bergman Bob" was the rage across America. "A beautiful cut," Bergman later admitted. With *Joan of Arc*, the Max Factor hair department completed the longest ongoing research job in its history—eight months and five days—to ensure the historical correctness of the wigs created for the film. Here Fred Frederick trims Ingrid Bergman's hair for *Joan of Arc*.

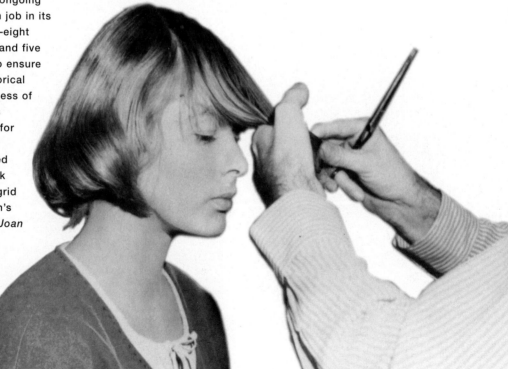

Errol Flynn was rated by Hollywood make-up artists as the most perfect type for wearing chin whiskers.

One of Jack Benny's hairpieces was seemingly delayed in transit between Max Factor's Hollywood studio and the Los Angeles theater where Benny was appearing on stage. It wasn't the delivery boy's fault. He had arrived at the theater early and, finding the front door closed, returned to Hollywood with the hairpiece. (He never thought to check the stage door, which was open.) Benny wasn't upset. As always, he carried a spare with him.

Sophia Loren looks on as noted Paramount hairstylist Nellie Manley adjusts a Max Factor wig for Loren's much-publicized Hollywood debut in *Desire Under the Elms* (1958).

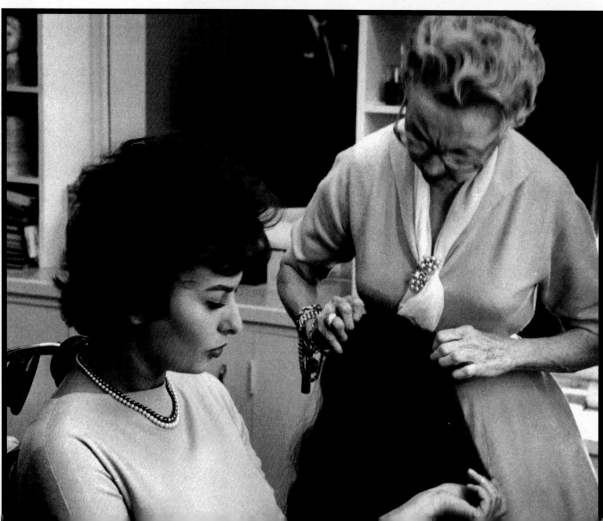

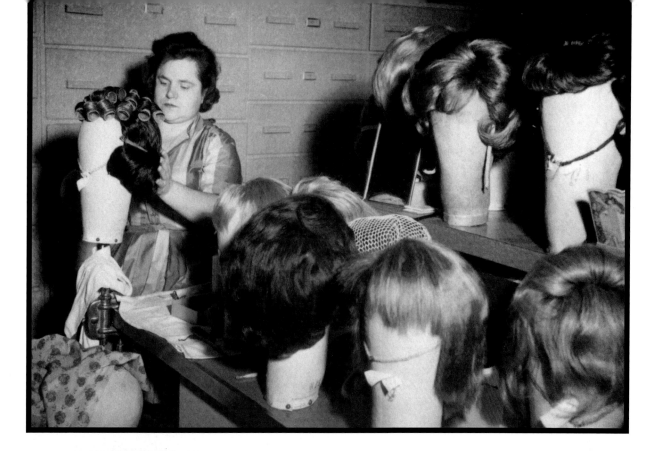

As an extension of its hair department, Max Factor introduced "Flatter Wigs," a collection of pre-styled wigs for women everywhere. The new wigs offered "a bewitchingly beautiful 60-second hairdo to suit every mood or whim—for fashion...for fun...daytime or evening...after swimming or going to a ball."
(Above) Flatter Wigs in various stages of styling are prepared in the Max Factor Hollywood salon.

Fred Frederick styles a new Flatter Wig on actress Jayne Mansfield. (The wig she is wearing can be seen on the second tier in the above photo.)

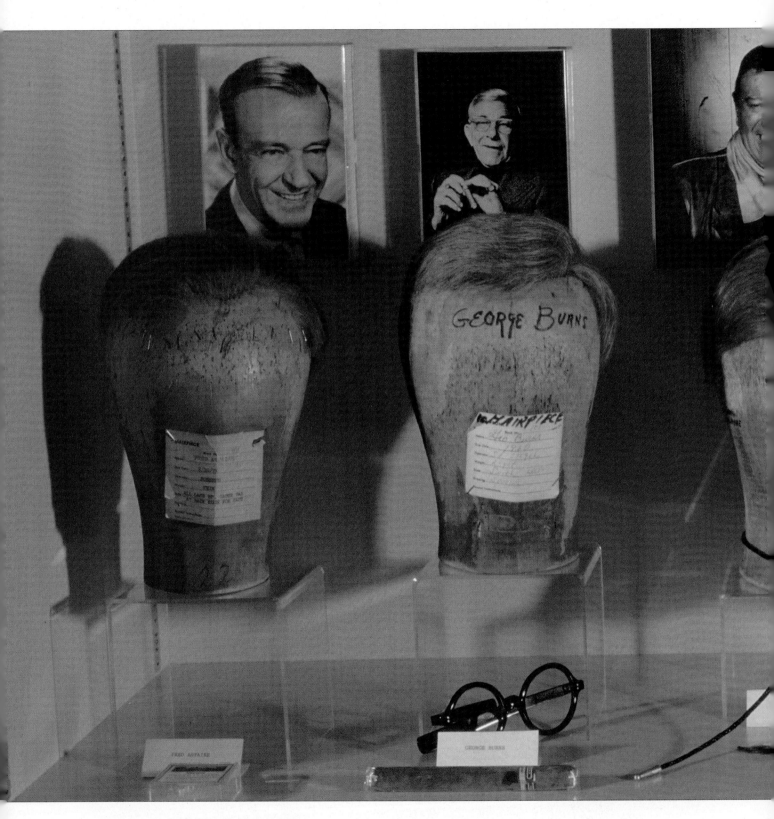

Max Factor-created celebrity toupees,
displayed on their wig blocks. Left to right:
Fred Astaire, George Burns, John Wayne,
James Stewart and Frank Sinatra.

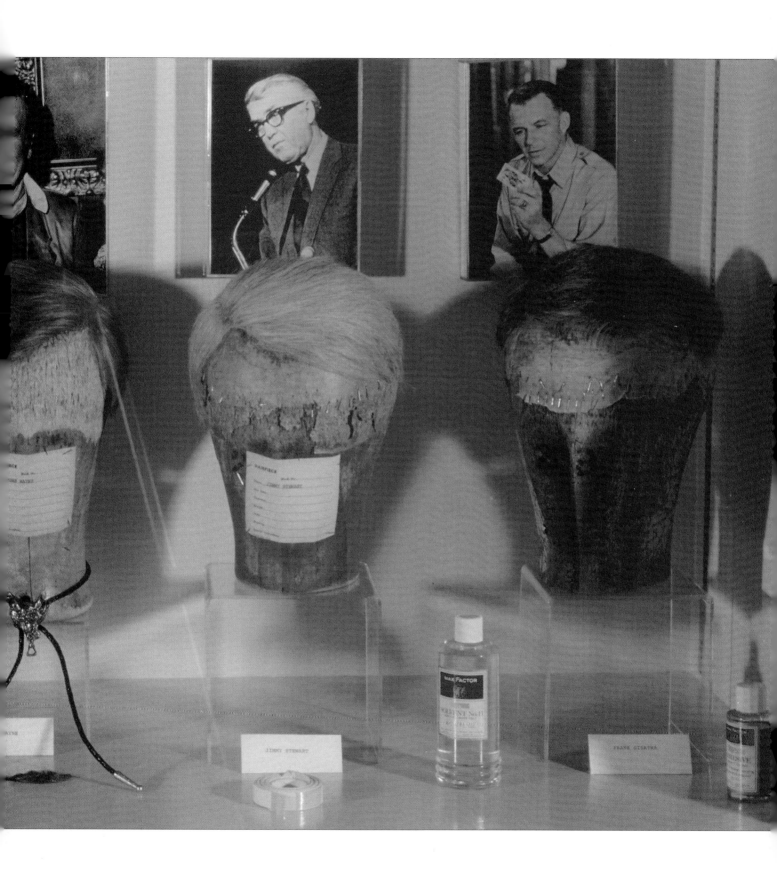

To Max Factor
a great Artist
Joan Crawford

Chapter 9

A World of Glamour

*I*n the years following World War II, Max Factor & Company began a worldwide expansion that few people, let alone the Factors, could have dreamed possible only a few years earlier. Factor branches had been established prior to the War in such countries as Great Britain, France, Canada and Cuba.

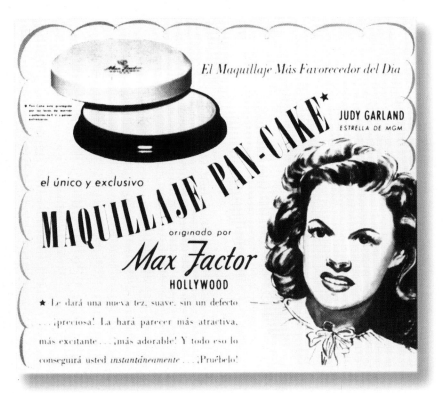

Spanish language ad featuring
Judy Garland, 1945.

Spanish language ad featuring
Rita Hayworth, 1946.

PARA ESTAR
MAS BONITA
Hoy
...y
Mañana

LANA TURNER
Estrella de MGM

Al maquillarse hoy, no deje de pensar en mañana. Recuerde que Maquillaje Pan-Cake, el famoso maquillaje de glamor originado por Max Factor Hollywood, no sólo le da, instantánea-mente, nuevo encanto para hoy, sino que su fórmula exclusiva y patentada protege su piel, evitando que se seque... y la mantiene suave, delicada y de aspecto juvenil. Pruébelo.

el único y exclusivo **MAQUILLAJE PAN-CAKE***

originado por

Max Factor Hollywood

En Todos Los Establecimientos
y Droguerías Principales

* Pan-Cake está protegido por las leyes de marcas y patentes de E. U. y países extranjeros.

Spanish language ad featuring
Lana Turner, 1945.

Now, thanks to the untiring energy of Board Chairman and CEO Davis Factor, the expansion moved to include Australia, South Africa, Ireland, Brazil, Italy, Japan, India and dozens more countries. By 1950, when Max Factor introduced its appropriately named "World of Beauty" make-up line, their products were available in 101 countries with branches circling the globe. The company provided employment for nearly 10,000 people worldwide.

The biggest post-war make-up news was the creation of "Pan-Stik," a cream make-up packaged in stick form. To use "Pan-Stik," it was necessary only to remove the cap and turn the revolving base until the make-up projected slightly from its case. The make-up was then stroked to the forehead, nose, cheeks and chin. Once blended with the fingertips over the entire face, it was powdered. "Pan-Stik" was described as non-oily and non-greasy. It was also called "fool proof," "amateur proof" and "streak proof."

Max Factor, Jr. with Don Lee at Lee's experimental television station in Hollywood, ca. 1946.

Like "Pan-Cake," "Pan-Stick" was created to meet specific motion picture needs, in this case the special lighting and photographic effects demanded for MGM's *That Forsyte Woman* (1949), starring Greer Garson, Errol Flynn and Walter Pidgeon. And, like "Pan-Cake," it was made available to the general public only after it had been used and tested to meet the demands of the screen.

"Pan-Stik" was the creation of Max Factor, Jr., who had conducted numerous tests and experiments long before *That Forsyte Woman* went into production. For his test subjects he worked with The Goldwyn Girls. He also persuaded personal friends to try it and let him observe the results. Said Max Jr., "Marguerite Chapman tested it for me in one of its very earliest forms. A little later, Jane Greer showed me its workings in a more perfected development. For olive complexion tones, Ava Gardner was my model. When it was nearly

As early as 1932, television had sufficiently proved itself as an exciting new medium that was here to stay. One of its biggest problems at that time, however, involved make-up. Max Factor and his son, Max Jr., aimed to solve those problems. Collaborative research was carried out with the Don Lee Los Angeles Experimental Television Station W6XAO. The resulting make-up line, coupled with new and different shades, was appropriately called "television make-up." The term was trademarked on June 6, 1933.

Additional research was interrupted by World War II, but in March, 1946, Max Factor announced his first perfected make-up created specifically for black-and-white television. Originally, a form of Panchromatic make-up had been used. It had worked then because the projected images from Iconoscope cameras were so poor, blurred by static, that the subjects were barely visible. Now, with a better camera and improved technology, a sharper

image was possible. Unfortunately, that image projected as a negative, sending out images in reverse. To help solve that problem, Max Factor, Jr. created a make-up that looked hideous in person, but once transmitted and reversed, looked normal. The thought of being photographed in this new television make-up petrified many actors. As strange as it looked, the make-up worked for a time.

In 1953, NBC and CBS television networks put out another call to Max Factor. When the two networks began their research to perfect color television, they discovered that existing make-up color was totally inadequate for this medium. Before the super-sensitive color cameras, the make-up appeared harsh, unflattering and unnatural. After seven months of extensive experiments and tests, Max Factor, Jr. finally perfected a complete new range of shades for color television, and on January 3, 1965, he delivered his new concept. As a result, the networks exclusively recommended to their own TV stations and affiliates Max Factor's "Color TV Make-Up" as the standard for all color television programs. Above: Early black-and-white television make-up.

Max Factor's make-up for
television.

perfected, Sylvia Sidney and Margaret Lindsey demonstrated its
advanced workings for me. And before 'Pan-Stik' was professionally
applied to Greer Garson, Errol Flynn or Walter Pidgeon for the film,
Lana Turner, Barbara Stanwyck, Judy Garland and Rosalind Russell
had to try it out. Where else but in Hollywood, and in what other
business but a make-up studio for the film industry, could anyone find
such famously beautiful and glamorous women to act as guinea pigs
for a new product?"

Greer Garson, star of MGM's *That Forsyte Woman*, 1949. "Pan-Stik" make-up was originated and perfected to meet the special lighting and photographic effects demanded by the film.

Max Factor's Hollywood make-up
studio at night with its glamorous
show windows, 1948.

Max Factor, Jr. worked with The Goldwyn Girls during 20 months of secret testing before launching "Pan-Stik" make-up. Part of the testing was done in sunlight on the roof of the Factor building in Hollywood, 1946.

Television was taking much of his time as well. With his father, he had begun initial research on television make-up as early as 1932. Twenty years later, additional research was needed, this time for color TV. Early on, television had not been a threat to motion pictures. Now it was, and the film industry was undergoing its own changes to combat TV's growing popularity.

Within the Factor organization there were changes, too. Three divisions—cosmetics, specialty (hairsprays, shampoos, pharmaceuticals) and sales—were merged into one. Each of the main divisions now had its own separate advertising, merchandising and sales departments. The number of sales personnel doubled, and the company acquired Parfums Corday, firmly establishing it in the fragrance business. Because of the unexpected economic recession of 1958, it took six months for sales and profits to catch up to the original forecasts. But the results were encouraging. Sales jumped from $7 million in 1958 to $57 million in 1959.

The company had reached its 50th anniversary. Ahead were even greater changes.

Revolutionary . . .

Different . . .

As Easy to Use as a Lipstick!

Pan-Stik
MAKE-UP

Originated by

Max Factor · Hollywood

. . . for those who

prefer a cream-type make-up

*Pan-Stik (trademark) means Max Factor Hollywood Cream-Type Make-Up.

A letter to Max Factor, Jr. from Natalie Kalmus, whose name appeared on the credits of every Technicolor film as Color Consultant through 1948, to acknowledge his gift to her of the new "Pan-Stik" make-up.

TECHNICOLOR MOTION PICTURE CORPORATION

HOLLYWOOD, CALIFORNIA

83½ ROMAINE STREET

HERBERT T KALMUS, PRESIDENT

October 14, 1948

Dear Mr. Factor:

You were indeed most thoughtful and gracious to send me the marvelous set of PAN-STIK. I was in the East at the time it arrived at my office and therefore have only now had the opportunity of trying out this new make-up.

I must say the PAN-STIK is the finest make-up I have ever used. It is certainly all that you claim it is, and more. My particular skin tones required my blending the medium with one of the lighter tones, as I found the medium just a tiny bit too dark. The best thing about having the group is that they do blend beautifully, and no doubt the medium shade would have been alright if I had had the proper face powder.

Believe me, I am most grateful for your generous gift and thank you most sincerely.

Cordially yours,

Natalie Kalmus

Natalie Kalmus
Color Director
TECHNICOLOR MOTION PICTURE CORP.

NK:lc

Mr. Max Factor, Jr.
1666 North Highland Avenue
Hollywood 28
California

Promotional photo of Ava Gardner, 1949. The accompanying descriptive copy read: "Ready for the Road. . . In the spring, Ava Gardner's fancy turns to motoring. And even though she drives with the top down on her convertible, Ava arrives at her destination neat and trim, because she has taken the necessary traveling beauty precautions beforehand. And once she applies her make-up, she always takes care to see that her eyebrows are brushed neatly back into place. The beautiful MGM actress will be seen opposite Van Heflin in *Upward to the Stars*." (The film's release title was *East Side West Side*.)

Ann Miller applies a new shade of lipstick as Max Factor, Jr. looks on. She later developed a passion for Factor's electric blue eye shadow, which was always kept in stock just for her. A cautioning sign on the shelf read, "Touch this and Ann Miller will tap dance all over your face!"

Her Majesty Queen Elizabeth personally visited the Max Factor display at the "Ideal Home Exhibition," 1951. The Queen is seen with (at left) Prince Philip, Viscountess Rothermere, and (at right) A.J. Kelin, managing director of Max Factor's British sales organization.

Crowds gather around the Max Factor exhibit at London's annual "Ideal Home Exhibition," 1951.

The American comedy team of Olsen and Johnson showed the crowd how not to apply make-up at the London trade show.

As early as 1930, Max Factor products were being seen in the windows of the world. Here, a lavish display window in Sydney, Australia, 1930. A branch of Max Factor & Co. was established in Australia in 1946.

(Below) Max Factor salon, Paris, 1952.

(Right) Max Factor Make-Up Studio, Havana, Cuba, 1953.

(Below) Max Factor display at the "Happy World Exhibition" in Singapore, 1952. Thousands of fascinated spectators watched demonstrations in the art of make-up.

Janet Leigh, who was starring with John Wayne in *Jet Pilot* (completed in 1950 but not released until 1957), was asked by Max Factor make-up artist Hal King to sit for a portrait as "the girl back home." It was King's concept of the ideal photo for a girl to send to her dearest boyfriend, particularly if he was in the armed forces and away from home. For the portrait, Leigh's hair was styled in "informal, soft and date-less simplicity." Her make-up too was simple but painstakingly done by King using "Pan-Stik" foundation. The only corrective make-up necessary was the extension of her eyebrow arch, just a fraction of an inch with eyebrow pencil.

Arlene Dahl demonstrates
Night Facial Stick, a new
night cream introduced by
Max Factor, early 1950s.

Gloria DeHaven, Barbara
Lawrence and Ann Miller
welcome Max Factor, Jr.
to the set of *Two Tickets
to Broadway*, 1951.

Ad, 1951.

Deborah Kerr shows how to use Pan-Cake make-up sponge, 1953.

Ad, 1951.

To commemorate Hollywood's Golden Anniversary, volunteer members of the Board of Directors of the Hollywood Chamber of Commerce, together with the motion picture, television and radio industries, created a $5 million exhibit called "Hollywood Historama," which included everything from the showing of old-time movies to props, costumes and memorabilia from Hollywood's past. One of the most popular attractions was Max Factor's "Beauty for the Entire World" with its collection of cosmetics, wigs and hairpieces. Photo: The Max Factor display at "Hollywood Historama."

Touring "Hollywood Historama's" exhibits, actress Coleen Gray and Max Factor, Jr. stop at blow-ups from *The Squaw Man*, the first film to use Max Factor's real hair wigs.

Teen-age Natalie Wood at the Max Factor
make-up salon, ca. 1955.

On January 11, 1955, Max Factor, Jr. (President) and Davis Factor (Chairman of the Board) broke ground for a new three-story $1 million general office/laboratory Max Factor building on North McCadden Place, directly behind the Highland Avenue building. It opened for business on February 11, 1956.

Joining Max Factor, Jr. and his wife, Millie, for an evening out are (l-r) Eddie Cantor, unidentified man, Mervyn LeRoy and George Burns, ca. 1957.

Ida Lupino, on behalf of the Academy of Television Arts and Sciences, presents the Academy's Distinguished Service Medallion to Max Factor, Jr. for his invaluable services to the television industry in the field of make-up for both black-and-white and color TV, ca. 1955.

Gladys Zender of Peru was crowned Miss Universe at the 1957 pageant, co-sponsored by Max Factor. The New Miss Universe, who stands to the left of Max Factor, Jr., became Factor's "Ambassadress of beauty" on a tour of Latin American countries. All contestants in the contest were guests at the Factor salon.

Promotional photo of Ann Blyth
for Max Factor mascara, ca. 1950.

Anne Jeffreys and Robert Sterling visit one of the labs with Max Factor, Jr., 1958.

The Factor factory at West Howe, Bournemouth, Hampshire, England, late 1950s. The panoramic view shows the Liquids Section of the Packaging Department, with the lipstick assembly belts in the foreground.

Hal King was Lucille Ball's long-time make-up man. During the early seasons of "I Love Lucy," the credits read, "Make-Up by Max Factor." The make-up was Max Factor, but it was King, Director of Beauty at the Hollywood salon, who gave Lucy her special look, whether it was knock-out gorgeous or just plain wacky. Before the end of the 1950s, the credits changed to "Make-Up by Hal King." But as Lucy's relationship with Desi Arnaz fell apart, so did her teaming with Hal King. She could not do without him, however. For her appearance in divorce court, she insisted on looking her very best, so once again she called upon Hal King. From then on, Lucille Ball was his primary client. King left Max Factor and Robert Salvatore was hired to replace him. Photo: Lucille Ball outside her "I Love Lucy" dressing room.

LUCILLE BALL ★

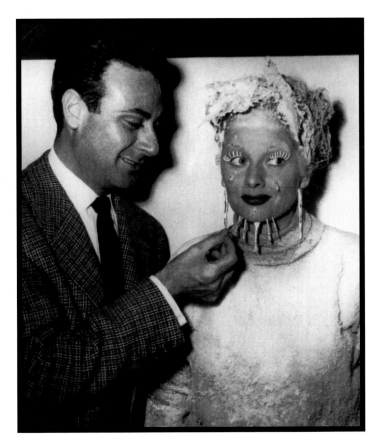

Hal King adds the finishing touch to Lucy's make-up for a comedic sketch.

Lum and Abner were so popular on radio that CBS brought them to television during the 1949–1950 season. The comedy team of Chester Lauck (Lum Edwards) and Norris Goff (Abner Peabody) ran the fictional Jot 'em Down General Store in Pine Bluff, Arkansas. It is doubtful they sold Max Factor make-up, but they wore it on TV.

Max Factor Jr. stands
alongside three-tiered
50th anniversary cake,
the centerpiece of
the company's
milestone event.

Francis X. Bushman and
celebrity look-alikes at the 50th
anniversary celebration.

Jayne Mansfield gets a smooch from Max Factor, Jr. as hubby Mickey Hargitay playfully objects during anniversary party.

Terry Moore joins hands with Max Factor, Jr. to congratulate him on the company's 50th anniversary, 1959.

MAX FACTO

Max Factor's star on Hollywood's "Walk of Fame" is located at 6922 Hollywood Boulevard. It was dedicated on February 9, 1969.

Chapter 10

Hollywood Legend

$\mathcal{A}$s Max Factor & Co. moved into the 1960s, mergers were becoming the rage in the United States. Factor was not only a target, but a hunter. One of the company's casting longing glances at the Factor organization was American Cyanamid. An agreement in principle to merge was reached, but the Factors decided against it at the last minute.

Toward the end of the 1960s, however, began a series of changes within the executive ranks of the organizational structure. Sidney Factor, youngest son of Max Factor, Sr., announced that he was going to devote his energies to his own personal enterprises. Barbara Factor, daughter of board chairman Davis Factor, left to be a full-time housewife. Donald Factor, son of Max Factor, Jr., left to fulfill his longtime ambition to become a motion picture producer. And Davis Factor, Jr. resigned to go into business for himself.

A new generation of leadership: (l-r) Donald Factor, Max Firestein, Chester Firestein, Alfred Firestein, Max Factor, Jr., Davis Factor and Louis Factor, ca 1961.

It seemed destined for Alfred and Chester Firestein, grandsons of Max, Sr., and the sole remaining members of the third generation, to head the company. In January, 1968, the Board of Directors elected Alfred Firestein, 43, President and Chief Executive Officer of Max Factor & Co., and Chester Firestein, 37, Executive Vice President and a member of the Executive Committee.

Davis Factor remained as Board Chairman, but relinquished his duties as CEO. Max Factor, Jr., former president, became Vice Chairman of the Board. Max Firestein, former Vice Chairman of the Board, became Chairman of the Executive Committee.

Sandra Dee pretends to wrap
Max Factor gift products for
a holiday promotion, late 1960s.

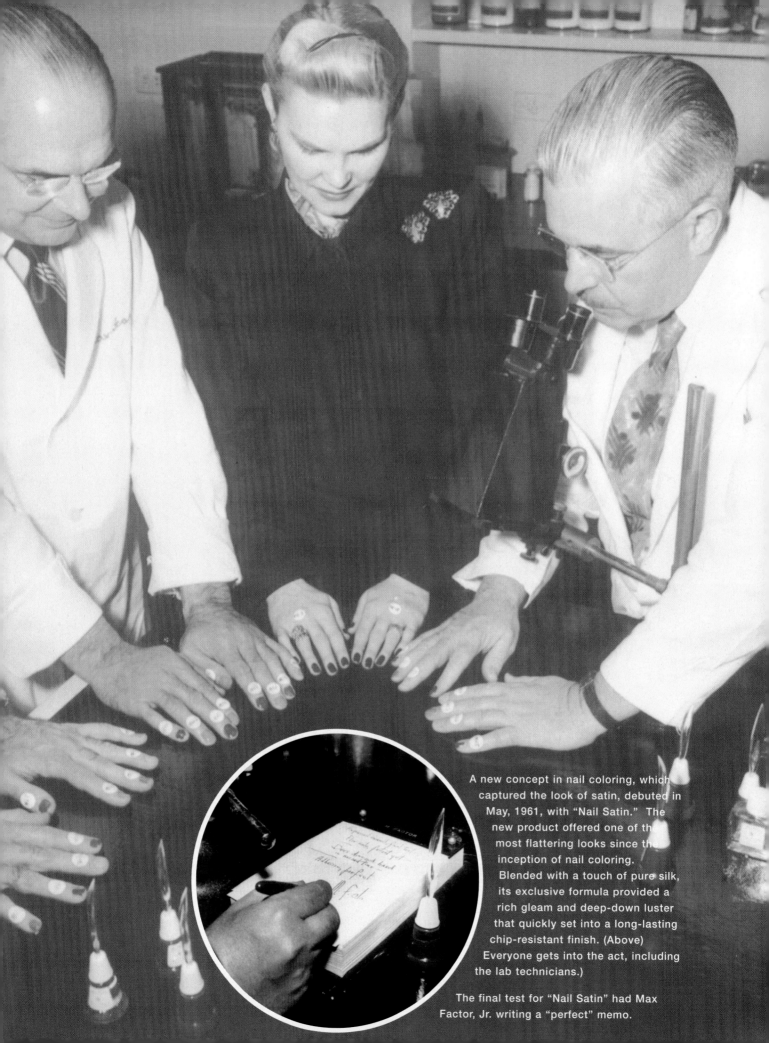

A new concept in nail coloring, which captured the look of satin, debuted in May, 1961, with "Nail Satin." The new product offered one of the most flattering looks since the inception of nail coloring. Blended with a touch of pure silk, its exclusive formula provided a rich gleam and deep-down luster that quickly set into a long-lasting chip-resistant finish. (Above) Everyone gets into the act, including the lab technicians.)

The final test for "Nail Satin" had Max Factor, Jr. writing a "perfect" memo.

Arlene Dahl demonstrates "Nail Satin."

Before she replaced Farrah Fawcett in "Charlie's Angels" (1978),
Cheryl Ladd posed with such Max Factor products as
"UltraLucent Nail Color."

Over the years, the Max Factor salon took on many looks, generally keyed to the seasons. Above and below: Spring and Autumn, 1960s...

I n acknowledging the responsibilities of his new position, Alfred Firestein paid tribute to the second generation members of the family for their aggressive leadership down through the years. "They have made this company one of the largest in the industry internationally," he said. "They built a business to heights that have far surpassed the loftiest dreams and expectations of its founder."

Soon after Alfred Firestein was elected president, he met David J. Mahoney, Chairman of the Board of Norton Simon, Inc. From the beginning, the two men had a great rapport. In 1972, merger negotiations were started with the Simon group. Completed

Natalie Wood applies Max Factor
"Creme Puff" near the entrance to
the salon, ca 1962.

Master chemist Lynn Gale (right) with Max Factor, Jr., whose sense of smell was so acute he became known as "the nose."

on February 14, 1973, the merger led Norton Simon, Inc. past fellow conglomerates Bristol Myers, General Foods, Johnson & Johnson, B.F. Goodrich, Pepsico, Nabisco and CBS with yearly earnings surpassing $1.1 billion.

Less than two months later, Alfred Firestein died at the age of 48. In November, 1973, David Mahoney appointed Chester Firestein president of Max Factor & Co. Under Chester Firestein's leadership, the company moved to new highs in both sales and earnings. Overseas markets expanded to include more than 200,000 accounts in 144 countries spanning the free world, led by Japan and the United Kingdom. New products were launched as well, most notably Halston designer fragrance.

Three years after his appointment to the presidency of Max Factor & Co., Chester Firestein resigned to devote his time to growing personal business activities. Over the next seven years, the company was to know three different presidents, all brought in from the outside to mastermind the business. In 1983, just as operations were beginning to run smoothly again under the leadership of Linda Wachner, Norton Simon, Inc. was taken over by Esmark. One year later, Esmark merged with Beatrice Companies, which made Max Factor an extension of its International Playtex Division. With the acquisition, the company

Joey Heatherton draws attention to Jet Perfume for a Christmas, 1961, promotion. Earlier in the year Max Factor & Co. had acquired all the outstanding capital stock of Parfumeri International Corday, Paris; Parfums Corday, Inc., New York and subsidiary corporations. (Since 1921, Parfums Corday, Inc. and its affiliates had created such famous French perfumes as Toujours Moi, Fame, Trapeze and Jet.)

Jaclyn Smith (below, left), one of the original stars of "Charlie's Angels," became an official spokesperson for the Max Factor fragrance, "Eprés", in 1981. (It was not her first teaming with the Factor company. Ten years earlier, she had been featured in several commercials for its beauty products.) For Smith, who had twice been voted by the readers of *People* magazine "the most beautiful woman in America" (1978, 1979), the Eprés association with Max Factor would not be her last. In 1989, she introduced for Max Factor "Jaclyn Smith's California." It was not only "the fragrance that captures the dream," as the ads noted, but the best women's fragrance of the year, according to the Fragrance Foundation.

To introduce its new fragrance, "Le Jardin de Max Factor," British actress Jane Seymour (below) was signed in 1983 to a three-year contract. "They say romance is back in style," said Seymour in the 30-second spot commercials. "I say it never went out." The flowery scent was the basis for the romantic campaign. (The following year, "Le Jardin de Max Factor" won Fragrance Foundation awards for most successful women's fragrance, best national advertising campaign for women's fragrance and best women's fragrance packaging.")

The Doris and Louis Factor Health Science Building (below, right), located on the UCLA campus in Los Angeles, houses research facilities, including the Department of Internal Medicine and the School of Nursing, the Jonsson Comprehensive Cancer Center, Hammer-Occidental Petroleum Laboratories and the McCarthy Biocontainment Laboratories. Endowed by the Factors, the complex was dedicated in 1981.

Ann and Davis Factor (lower right) greet friends during an evening out, late 1960s. Davis was a two-term President of the National Toilet Goods Association and, for many years, the only man away from the New York area to hold that office.

headquarters was moved to Stamford, Connecticut. Despite all the changes, Max Factor earned its second Fragrance Foundation Award for its newly introduced "Le Jardin de Max Factor."

The public knew little of what was taking place behind the scenes until the beautiful salon on the main floor of the Factor building was ordered closed. No longer could customers walk in for make-up consultations and treatment. A smaller retail store with an adjoining beauty shop was opened in the space once occupied by the hair department, but it was not as spacious or nearly as classy.

Beautiful Cristina Ferrare introduced Max Factor's "Ultra Lucent Waterproof Make-Up" in mid-1971. The new make-up was developed "to stay on perfectly under all conditions —even an underwater swim."

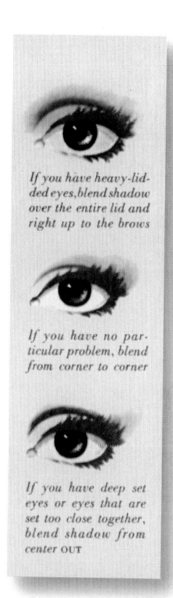

If you have heavy-lid-ded eyes, blend shadow over the entire lid and right up to the brows

If you have no particular problem, blend from corner to corner

If you have deep set eyes or eyes that are set too close together, blend shadow from center OUT

If the 1980s called for a return to romance, can a return to glamour be far behind? Without question, today's trend is to glamour, a flashback to the glorious, glamorous days of the 1940s and 1950s, exemplified by such stars as Grace Kelly, Ava Gardner, Audrey Hepburn, Marilyn Monroe, Rita Hayworth and so many others. Here (and opposite) are Max Factor's secrets of the stars, his make-up tips for the glamorous woman of 1955.

It was the suggestion of Beauty Director Robert Salvatore to turn the original salon and make-up rooms into a museum. Working with the staff and family members, he obtained hundreds of historic items of interest for display, including wigs and hairpieces worn by the stars in their film roles, make-up samples and other Factor-originated beauty innovations. The Max Factor Museum opened in time to lure visitors attending the 1984 Olympic Games in Los Angeles. It soon became a major Hollywood attraction.

In 1986, Kohlberg, Kravis, Roberts & Company generated one of Wall Street's most complex deals with its acquisition of Beatrice Companies. An adjunct to these negotiations involved International Playtex, of which Max Factor was a subsidiary. Kohlberg, Kravis, Roberts sold the Playtex division and its subsidiaries to Joel Smilow, an Esmark/Beatrice executive. Smilow retained Playtex but sold its beauty division to Revlon's Ron Perelman. Max Factor was now part of the family that included Almay, Charles of the Ritz, Germaine Monteil, Alexandra de Markoff and Visage Beaute.

The following year, Ron Perelman placed his confidence in Neutrogena's former President of Consumer Products, Allan Kurtzman. Kurtzman accepted the position as President of Max Factor worldwide with the stipulation that the company return to its former headquarters in Los Angeles.

Kurtzman was no stranger to the Factor organization. He had first worked for the company in the 1960s when Alfred Firestein appointed him Corporate Vice President and Director of U.S. marketing. Caught in the crossfire of the Norton Simon merger, he left disheartened.

In 1988, a handful of surviving employees returned to California filled with hope. Kurtzman assembled an energetic work force of top industry talent, and his direction of the company received a boost when, in 1990, Max Factor garnered its third Fragrance Foundation Award for the mass marketing success of "Jaclyn Smith's California." (Promotion had taken on a new look, starting in 1968, with the use of professional models. The first to be featured was Cristina Ferrare, who was seen in more commercials and print ads than any other feature model to that time. Other young Hollywood hopefuls who won Factor auditions were Cheryl Ladd, Farrah Fawcett, Bo Derek, Veronica Hamel, Shari Belafonte, Cheryl Tiegs, Jane Seymour and, of course, Jaclyn Smith.)

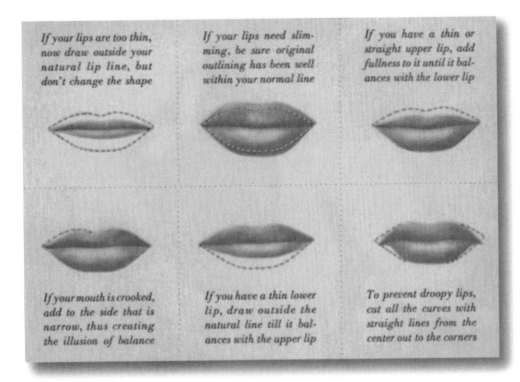

If your lips are too thin, now draw outside your natural lip line, but don't change the shape

If your lips need slimming, be sure original outlining has been well within your normal line

If you have a thin or straight upper lip, add fullness to it until it balances with the lower lip

If your mouth is crooked, add to the side that is narrow, thus creating the illusion of balance

If you have a thin lower lip, draw outside the natural line till it balances with the upper lip

To prevent droopy lips, cut all the curves with straight lines from the center out to the corners

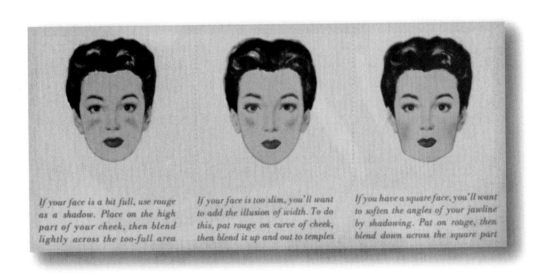

If your face is a bit full, use rouge as a shadow. Place on the high part of your cheek, then blend lightly across the too-full area

If your face is too slim, you'll want to add the illusion of width. To do this, pat rouge on curve of cheek, then blend it up and out to temples

If you have a square face, you'll want to soften the angles of your jawline by shadowing. Pat on rouge, then blend down across the square part

When I first moved to Los Angeles in 1980 and signed with the Nina Blanchard modeling agency, I was sent to Max Factor's make-up studio in Hollywood. I'd never really worn make-up before, but Bob Salvatore showed me what to do and what to use. He really taught me everything about make-up. Then I did a photo session for a print ad. Few companies were using black models at that time, but Max Factor's took a chance with me. It was my first break in Hollywood.

—Shari Belafonte

Best Wishes!
Jaclyn Smith

Jaclyn Smith with Max
Factor's Director of Beauty,
Robert Salvatore.

Yet another change was in the offing. In 1991, Max Factor was taken over by Procter & Gamble and, once again, the executive offices were headed east, this time to Cincinnati, Ohio. While the future of the historic Factor building in Hollywood is uncertain, the doors of the Max Factor Museum remain open as a tribute to Hollywood's master of make-up. But his accomplishments will live on for generations wherever movies are shown—in theaters, on television, videocassettes and laser discs. The number of his creative innovations are almost impossible to list.

Without Max Factor, the great faces that filled the movie screens would not be as adored or as memorable, and cosmetics would not exist as we know them today. He didn't invent glamour, but he certainly made it popular and, in doing so, he brought it within the reach of women everywhere. With his gift of glamour to the movies, he changed the faces of the world.

And the legend continues...

Internationally famous architect S. Charles Lee (center) meets in 1991 with co-author Robert Salvatore (right) and Max Factor building property manager, Kenneth Gamble, to review his original architectural plans from 1935. It was Mr. Lee who redesigned the entire facility that has since become a Hollywood landmark.

The main salon at the Max Factor Museum of Beauty in 1995 looked much as it did when it opened 60 years earlier, thanks to Jack Nicholson. It was Nicholson who arranged to have the room brought back to its near-original Art Deco splendor for interiors in his film, *The Two Jakes* (1990). The exterior had been used in 1987 as the facade of a jewelry store robbed by Brigitte Nielsen in *Beverly Hills Cop II*.

Historic photos and memorabilia on display at the Max Factor Museum of Beauty in Hollywood, 1994.

Early logo for Max Factor Museum was based on a design used following the move to Hollywood from downtown Los Angeles in 1928.

The Gibson Girl

The Gibson Girl was the idealized American image at the turn of the century. Women of the day were fastidiously groomed. Hair was brushed every evening until it gleamed, then wrapped on top of the head. Cosmetics were seldom worn, especially in public during the day. A woman might pinch her cheeks for a little color, and bite her lips. If she dared, she took pigmented tissue-like paper, wet it and applied it to her cheek and lips. She might even have used berries or pure vegetable food coloring, but for evening only. High society women dabbled more in heavy creams and powders, and made themselves up for evening theater or the opera.

1900-1909

The Gibson Girl
Lillian Russell
Lillie Langtry
Florence Lawrence

Mary Pickford

Theda Bara

Women began wearing minimal theatrical make-up to look more like their favorite "moving picture" stars. Powder was still the cosmetic of choice, fluffed onto faces with huge swansdown puffs, smothering even eyebrows and lashes in white dust. The effect was very blank and pale. Max Factor's "bee stung" lips were coming into fashion.

1910-1919

Theda Bara
Gloria Swanson
Mae Marsh
Betty Compson
Lillian Gish
Bebe Daniels
Mary Pickford
Marguerite Clark
Norma Talmadge
Alice Joyce
Blanche Sweet
Polly Moran
Pola Negri
Constance Talmadge
Mary Miles Minter
Dorothy Dalton
Louise Fazenda
Ruth Roland
Renee Adoree
Clara Kimball Young
Irene Rich
Mabel Normand
Geraldine Farrar

Max Factor's Gallery Of Glamour

Mae Murray

Dolores Costello
Alla Nazimova
Corinne Griffith
Gloria Swanson
Joan Crawford
Pola Negri
Madge Bellamy
Leatrice Joy
Clara Bow
Carole Lombard
Mae Murray
Barbara LaMarr
Mae Bush
Greta Garbo
Marion Davies
Myrna Loy
Renee Adoree
Billie Dove
Vilma Banky

1920-1929

Carole Lombard

More adventurous women greased their eyelids with vaseline and wore cake mascara or eyelash beading; plus a little rouge, which tended to look quite severe. Eyeshadow was scarce and was available only in gray (later brown, then blue). Few women wore lipstick or pomade. Pink and white lipsalves were seen at times. The very daring wore crimson lips to look like Clara Bow. It was either no color or boldly artificial color. Women were given "Complexion Analysis" cards, then prescribed the correct colors of powder, powder foundation, rouge and lip colors to match their hair, face and eye coloring. For the first time, women were not buying blindly.

Merle Oberon

1930-1939

Jean Harlow
Marlene Dietrich
Dolores Del Rio
Ginger Rogers
Joan Crawford
Greta Garbo
Carole Lombard
Loretta Young
Katharine Hepburn
Mae West
Madeleine Carroll
Merle Oberon
Hedy Lamarr
Norma Shearer
Sally Rand
Gypsy Rose Lee
Jeanette MacDonald

Marlene Dietrich

Eyebrows were shaved or severely tweezed and penciled in. Bleach mask was introduced to eliminate suntans or skin discolorations. Lipsticks and eyeshadows were available in more colors. Pan-Cake make-up, created for Technicolor films, became the first full face make-up foundation.

Dolores Del Rio

Jeanne Crain

Ann Sheridan

Suzy Parker

1940-1949

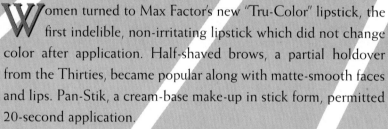

Lauren Bacall

Marilyn Monroe

Women turned to Max Factor's new "Tru-Color" lipstick, the first indelible, non-irritating lipstick which did not change color after application. Half-shaved brows, a partial holdover from the Thirties, became popular along with matte-smooth faces and lips. Pan-Stik, a cream-base make-up in stick form, permitted 20-second application.

Hedy Lamarr
Lana Turner
Rita Hayworth
Ann Sheridan
Linda Darnell
Ann Sothern
Madeleine Carroll
Vivien Leigh
Gene Tierney
Jeanne Crain
Ava Gardner
Cyd Charisse
Betty Grable
Virginia Mayo
Lauren Bacall
Maureen O'Hara
Lena Horne

1950-1959

Grace Kelly
Kim Novak
Marilyn Monroe
Elizabeth Taylor
Sophia Loren
Brigitte Bardot
Ava Gardner
Suzy Parker
Jean Simmons
Arlene Dahl

Kim Novak

Brigitte Bardot

New products created by Max Factor began a cosmetics revolution. The "Secret Key" skincare line was the first of its kind to be totally moisturized. Erase, a new type of coverup, eliminated discolorations that foundation could not hide. Loose powder sales all but disappeared with the debut of "Creme Puff." And the introduction of countless new shades of eye color (powder and cream eyeshadows, mascara wands, eyebrow pencils with refills and false eyelashes) set the stage for the color explosion in the coming decade.

Ursula Andress

Ann-Margret

Marilyn Monroe
Ann-Margret
Raquel Welch
Ursula Andress
Elizabeth Taylor
Natalie Wood
Capucine
Candice Bergen
Sophia Loren
Julie Christie
Audrey Hepburn
Brigitte Bardot
Jean Shrimpton
Twiggy
Jeanne Moreau
Gina Lollobrigida

1960-1969

Make-up became stylized after the natural, fresh look of the Fifties. Fun, even bizarre looks were in. Young ladies painted their lips with Erase to make them appear lighter than their already pale faces. Hair went huge, bouffant, beehive. Eyes were smudged with all sorts of things, including "Wild White Shiny Eyeliner." Black, too, became the rage for a time, thanks to Elizabeth Taylor's "Cleopatra eyes."

Farrah Fawcett

Catherine Deneuve

Christie Brinkley

1970-1979

Catherine Deneuve
Ali MacGraw
Elizabeth Taylor
Farrah Fawcett
Candice Bergen
Cher
Beverly Johnson
Tookie Smith
Lauren Hutton
Cybill Shepherd
Cristina Ferrare
Jaclyn Smith

The Seventies marked the return to nature with fruits and vegetables making an appearance in a variety of skincare products, notably avocado and lemon. Popular make-up trends included soft and natural blushers, frosted highlighters beneath the brow and on the ball of the eyelid, bright lips and gloss.

Candice Bergen

Isabella Rossellini

Elizabeth Taylor

Cheryl Tiegs

Julia Roberts

Shari Belafonte

1980-1989

Brooke Shields
Iman
Cheryl Tiegs
Christie Brinkley
Isabella Rossellini
Madonna
Jane Seymour
Shari Belafonte
Jacqueline Bisset
Kathleen Turner
Michelle Pfeiffer
Bo Derek
Paulina

Brows, untweezed and natural, often brushed up. Liquid eyeline out, smudgable pencils in. Emphasis on lips and eyes. Big fashion statement: Invisible make-up.

Cindy Crawford

Sela Ward

Michelle Pfeiffer

1990-

Cindy Crawford
Linda Evangelista
Claudia Schiffer
Michelle Pfeiffer
Demi Moore
Julia Roberts
Naomi Campbell
Sharon Stone
Heather Locklear
Vanessa Williams
Sela Ward

Big, natural brows, even penciled to look larger. Shadows are earth toned—browns, melons, beiges—or very natural flesh tones. Big, matte lips and a return to liquid eyeliner. Tans are taboo; blushes fade from the scene.

Demi Moore

April 2, 1904	Arrived in America.
April 11, 1904	Opened concession at the St. Louis World's Fair.
October 11, 1908	Moved to Los Angeles.
January 2, 1909	Official date of the founding of the Max Factor business.
May 22, 1912	Became a United States citizen.
June 7, 1914	Perfected the first make-up specifically created for motion picture use.
January 20, 1915	Coined the word "brownette" for approximately 50% of all women who have brown hair that is "in between" blonde and brunette shades.
July 9, 1916	Introduced eye shadow and eyebrow pencil to his new "Society" make-up line.
February 3, 1917	Paramount's *Joan the Woman* became the first motion picture in which all make-up problems were considered and provided from the film's script before production began.
August 20, 1917	Introduced "make-up blender" for the first time as a glamorizing aid to women in general.
September 2, 1918	Developed the "Color Harmony" principle of make-up.
1919	Invented false eyelashes using human hair.
July 9, 1920	Began referring to his beautifying products as "make-up."
October 6, 1921	Created the "face powder brush."
January 23, 1925	Completed the greatest single make-up order of all time—more than 600 gallons of body make-up for *Ben Hur.*
October 7, 1927	First national distribution of "Max Factor Color Harmony Make-Up" products in the United States.
July 5, 1928	Created "Panchromatic Make-up" for motion pictures. (Trademarked December 11, 1928.)
April 13, 1928	Awarded special citation from the Academy of Motion Picture Arts and Sciences for his contribution to the success of Panchromatic film research conducted by the Academy.
June 8, 1928	Jean Harlow became a "platinum blonde," starting a new hair color craze and forcing development of new "Color Harmony" make-up shades.
1929	First use of celebrity endorsements.
February 24, 1930	Established export division.
March 23, 1930	Invented "lip gloss."
October 3, 1932	Developed first "television make-up." (Trademarked June 6, 1933.)
January 14, 1933	Invented "self-measure-and-chart" procedure for mail-order hairpieces.
November 26, 1935	Gala re-opening of Hollywood make-up studio.
December 16, 1937	Created "Pan-Cake" make-up for Technicolor films (with Max Factor, Jr.).
February 5, 1937	Opened London salon.
October 1, 1937	Established in France.
August 30, 1938	Max Factor, Sr. died.
February 1, 1940	Established in Manila.
February 17, 1940	Created "Tru-Color" lipstick.
April 17, 1940	Established in Canada.
May 1, 1941	Established in Cuba.
January 11, 1943	Developed camouflage make-up for U.S. Marine Corps.
October 1, 1944	Established in Mexico.
January 1, 1946	Established in Australia.
March 1946	Introduced first perfected make-up created specifically for black-and-white TV.
May 1, 1946	Established in South Africa.
October 1, 1946	Established in Argentina.
October 16, 1946	Completed the largest wig order of all time for *Forever Amber.*
December 14, 1946	Established in Brazil.

Max Factor
Milestones

July 1, 1947	Established in Ireland.
August 23, 1947	Created "Pan-Stik" make-up.
September 8, 1947	Completed the longest steady research job in the company's history for Joan of Arc.
July 28, 1948	Established in Italy.
March 15, 1950	Introduced "World of Beauty" line.
June 1, 1951	Introduced "Signature" line for men.
May 4, 1952	Introduced "Color-Fast" lipstick.
January 25, 1953	Introduced "Creme Puff" make-up.
July 1, 1953	Established in Japan.
January 3, 1954	Introduced a new concept in make-up for color television.
July 1, 1954	Introduced the original cover-up, "Erase," (developed for the movies) to the general public.
November 1, 1954	Introduced "Electrique," the company's first entry into the fragrance field.
April 4, 1955	Introduced "Hi-Fi Fluid Make-Up" as a direct result of extensive research for color television with the major networks.
August 16, 1956	Announced the purchase of all outstanding shares of Lee Limited, owner of the trademarks "Sof-Set" and "Dri-Mist."
September 10, 1956	Established in Sweden.
November 1, 1956	Introduced "Primitif" fragrance.
April 28, 1957	Introduced "Cup of Youth" moisturizing skin cream.
July 1957	First co-sponsored Miss Universe Beauty Pageant.
November 1, 1958	Introduced "Hypnotique" fragrance.
November 23, 1958	Introduced first automatic refillable mascara, "Mascara Wand."
January 2, 1959	50th anniversary of Max Factor & Co.
April 1, 1959	Established in Germany.
March 2, 1960	Introduced "California Sun Colors."
May 2, 1960	Introduced "Iridescent Mascara Wand."

June 26, 1960	Introduced "Cool Coffee Colors."
July 15, 1960	Opened new salon in Rome.
September 15, 1960	Introduced "Basic Black" eye shadow.
September 20, 1960	Opened modern cosmetic factory and general offices in Milan, Italy.
October 3, 1960	Introduced "Sheer Genius" liquid make-up.
December 27, 1960	Introduced "Swedish Formula" hand cream.
March 1, 1961	Introduced no-shine lipsticks in "California Sun Pastels."
April 19, 1961	Listed for the first time on the New York Stock Exchange.
May 1, 1961	Introduced "Nail Satin."
July 1, 1961	Acquired all outstanding capital stock of Parfumeri Internationale Corday.
June 3, 1963	Received Hollywood Advertising Club's Founder's Award.
September 1964	Introduced "Max Factor for Gentlemen."
October 1964	Introduced "Royal Regiment" line for men.
April 1965	Introduced "UltraLucent" make-up line.
December 1965	Introduced "Geminesse" total skin-care line.
October 1966	Introduced "Promesse" fragrance.
1968	Began use of professional models in ads.
July 1971	Introduced "UltraLucent" waterproof make-up.
February 14, 1973	Merged with Norton Simon Inc.
May 1974	Introduced "Wigless Wig" to Flatter Wig collection.
February 1975	Introduced the Halston line of fragrance products.
May 1976	Introduced "Pure Moisture" line.
1984	Acquired by Beatrice Companies.
	Opened Max Factor Museum.
1986	Acquired by Ron Perelman/Revlon.
1991	Acquired by Procter & Gamble.

Index